Guest-edited by
FLORA SAMUEL and ELI HATLESKOG

Social Value
in Architecture

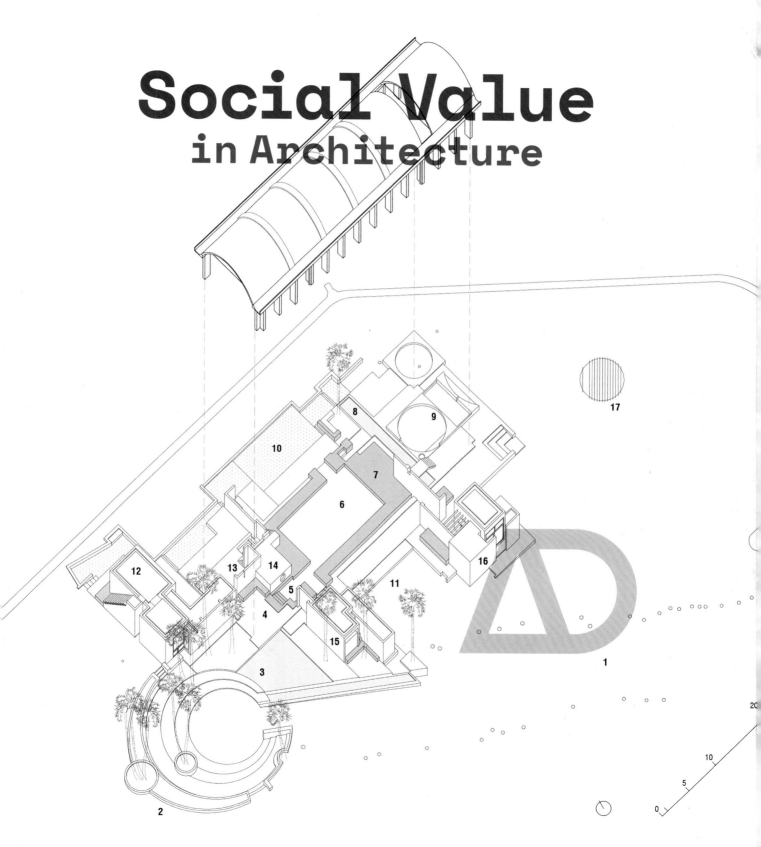

AART Architects, VUC Syd, Haderslev, Denmark, 2013

MESA community mapping event, Orts Road Estate, Reading, 2019

ISSN 0003-8504
ISBN 978 1119 576440

Edward Ng, Li Wan, Xinan Chi and Wenfeng Bai,
Prototype house for Guangming village
post-earthquake reconstruction,
The Chinese University of Hong Kong and
Kunming University of Science and Technology,
2016

Taylor and Hinds Architects, krakani lumi,
wukalina-Mount William National Park,
Tasmania,
2018

Editorial Offices
John Wiley & Sons
9600 Garsington Road
Oxford
OX4 2DQ

T +44 (0)1865 776868

Editor
Neil Spiller

Commissioning Editor
Helen Castle

Managing Editor
Caroline Ellerby
Caroline Ellerby Publishing

Freelance Contributing Editor
Abigail Grater

Publisher
Paul Sayer

Art Direction + Design
CHK Design:
Christian Küsters
Barbara Nassisi

Production Editor
Elizabeth Gongde

Prepress
Artmedia, London

Printed in Italy by Printer
Trento Srl

Journal Customer Services
For ordering information,
claims and any enquiry
concerning your journal
subscription please go to
www.wileycustomerhelp
.com/ask or contact your
nearest office.

Americas
E: cs-journals@wiley.com
T: +1 781 388 8598 or
+1 800 835 6770 (toll free
in the USA & Canada)

**Europe, Middle East
and Africa**
E: cs-journals@wiley.com
T: +44 (0)1865 778315

Asia Pacific
E: cs-journals@wiley.com
T: +65 6511 8000

Japan (for Japanese-
speaking support)
E: cs-japan@wiley.com
T: +65 6511 8010 or 005 316
50 480 (toll-free)

Visit our Online Customer
Help available in 7 languages
at www.wileycustomerhelp
.com/ask

Print ISSN: 0003-8504
Online ISSN: 1554-2769

Prices are for six issues
and include postage and
handling charges. Individual-
rate subscriptions must be
paid by personal cheque or
credit card. Individual-rate
subscriptions may not be
resold or used as library
copies.

All prices are subject to
change without notice.

Identification Statement
Periodicals Postage paid
at Rahway, NJ 07065.
Air freight and mailing in
the USA by Mercury Media
Processing, 1850 Elizabeth
Avenue, Suite C, Rahway,
NJ 07065, USA.

USA Postmaster
Please send address changes
to *Architectural Design*,
John Wiley & Sons Inc.,
c/o The Sheridan Press,
PO Box 465, Hanover,
PA 17331, USA

Rights and Permissions
Requests to the Publisher
should be addressed to:
Permissions Department
John Wiley & Sons Ltd
The Atrium
Southern Gate
Chichester
West Sussex PO19 8SQ
UK

F: +44 (0)1243 770 620
E: Permissions@wiley.com

Subscribe to D
D is published bimonthly
and is available to purchase
on both a subscription basis
and as individual volumes
at the following prices.

Prices
Individual copies:
£29.99 / US$45.00
Individual issues on
D App for iPad:
£9.99 / US$13.99
Mailing fees for print
may apply

Annual Subscription Rates
Student: £90 / US$137
print only
Personal: £136 / US$215
print and iPad access
Institutional: £310 / US$580
print or online
Institutional: £388 / US$725
combined print and online
6-issue subscription on
D App for iPad: £44.99 /
US$64.99

ARCHITECTURAL DESIGN

July/August	Profile No.
2020	**266**

Disclaimer
The Publisher and Editors cannot be held responsible
for errors or any consequences arising from the use
of information contained in this journal; the views and
opinions expressed do not necessarily reflect those of
the Publisher and Editors, neither does the publication
of advertisements constitute any endorsement by
the Publisher and Editors of the products advertised.

Flora Samuel

Eli Hatleskog

Note

1. This work was supported by an Institutional Links grant ID 332241573, under the Newton Philippines partnership. The grant is funded by the UK Department of Business, Energy and Industrial Strategy (BEIS) and CHED, and delivered by the British Council. For further information, please visit www.newtonfund.ac.uk.

Social value and its relationship to the environment have been long-term interests for Guest-Editors Eli Hatleskog and Flora Samuel. The climate change emergency and social inequality cannot be addressed without changing the way in which 'value' is framed in the built environment. Both editors believe in working across interdisciplinary boundaries and have a shared interest in bringing forth the viewpoints of those whose voices are rarely heard in discussions about architecture, planning and construction.

Hatleskog joined Samuel, a Professor at the University of Reading, as a researcher on the Mapping Eco-Social Assets (MESA) institutional links project she leads, which is funded by the British Council in collaboration with the University of Santo Tomas in Manila, the Philippines.[1] Since the project's inception in April 2018, the importance of mapping and measuring social value in emergent nations has quickly become apparent. Robust, transparent evidence is urgently needed in countries such as the Philippines to make a case against inappropriate project proposals, often by overseas investors with no interest in preserving communities or the environment. In this way social value can play a major role in delivering the Sustainable Development Goals (SDGs) and restoring faith in the social contract between people and decision-makers.

Before moving to the University of Reading to assist Lorraine Farrelly in the setting up of its new Architecture School, Samuel was head of the University of Sheffield School of Architecture. It was here that she was immersed in the political and environmental potential of socially oriented architecture practice, a subject she explored in her book *Why Architects Matter* (Routledge, 2018) and through her role as the first RIBA Vice President for Research. She argues that the marginalisation of architects from the production of the built environment is due to the difficulty in demonstrating their value in a manner that other disciplines can understand – hence the need to promote research in practice.

While investigating methods for mapping intangible assets at Reading, Hatleskog has also been on the Urban Integrated Diagnostics team at the University of Bristol, where she is exploring how creative practice research can benefit transdisciplinary urban research and has developed visual methods to support the city's One City Approach. Prior to this she was part of Architecture, Design and Art Practice Training-research, an EU Innovative Training Network studying models and methodologies for creative-practice doctoral research across Europe. Through her activities, she explores how architectural research can encourage more joined-up and inclusive approaches to the environment.

For Hatleskog and Samuel, an ability to capture social value, to generate appropriate design, promote shared learning and enable informed decision-making will be vital for the next generation of architects. This can only be achieved in cultural collaboration with other disciplines and as a conversation between universities and practice. This issue of Δ, simultaneously a source of inspiration and a call to action, brings together a range of pioneering work in this area. Δ

Why Social Value?

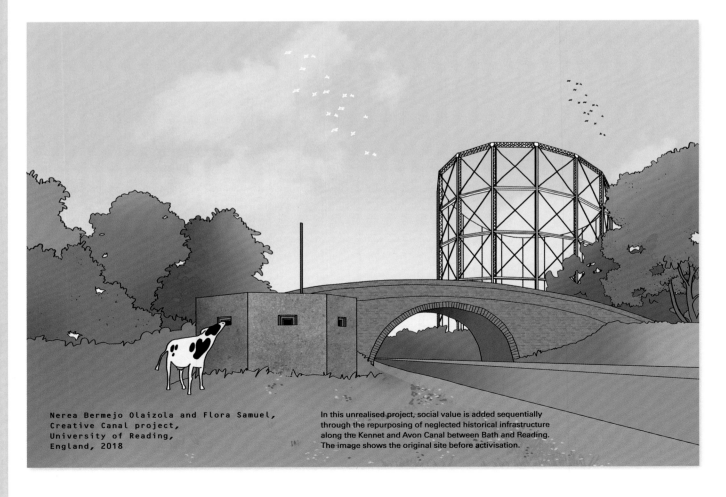

Nerea Bermejo Olaizola and Flora Samuel,
Creative Canal project,
University of Reading,
England, 2018

In this unrealised project, social value is added sequentially
through the repurposing of neglected historical infrastructure
along the Kennet and Avon Canal between Bath and Reading.
The image shows the original site before activisation.

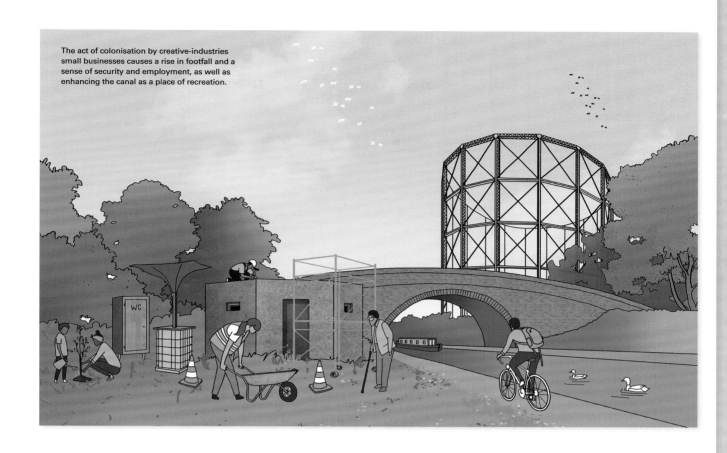

The act of colonisation by creative-industries small businesses causes a rise in footfall and a sense of security and employment, as well as enhancing the canal as a place of recreation.

Some of the potential social value generated by the repurposing of 19th-century infrastructure for 21st-century industry and community.

As societies face impending challenges relating to climate change, densification and social upheaval, now is an opportune moment to discuss what we value most and how architects and architecture can play a role in improving people's lives. If architects are to reverse their current trajectory into the margins of an increasingly 'lean' and economically driven construction sector, it is important to reflect on the value of architectural design. This issue of ⌀ explores the meaning and potential of social value as an instrument of change in the built environment.

It includes a range of case studies from across the globe of architects who are developing methodologies for creating, measuring and mapping social value, arguably the most intangible and important impact of architectural activity. The first two articles, by Karen Kubey (pp 14–21) and Peter Sattrup (pp 22–9), provide important contextual reviews of the social value scene in the US and Denmark, respectively. The following contributions explore the mapping and measuring of the social value of communities using different methodologies and media that converge on its cultural dimension, and the concluding articles act as a timely reminder that social value is a neoliberal construct that does not necessarily translate to authentic cultures of respect and love.

Baseco,
Manila,
The Philippines,
2016

below: Children sifting through waterborne rubbish in floodwater caused by extreme weather conditions. Architects and architecture can assist in alleviating these conditions.

bottom: The devastating social and environmental impact of climate change on communities. Architects have an ethical duty to consider the impact of their actions on people near and far.

Valuation

'If we cannot define what we mean by value, we cannot be sure to produce it, nor to share it fairly, nor to sustain economic growth.'[1] The economist Mariana Mazzucato provides a compelling critique of valuation practices across the globe, making an important distinction between value creation (for example, the work of the public sector for public good) and value extraction (financial gain from the trading of stocks and shares). 'Value' is a contradictory word. Like the architectural concept of 'transparency', it can be a tool for accountability and inclusion, but also a medium of control. Where value is mentioned, audit follows, and this always begins with classification – a 'powerful' technology that is both 'political and ethical'.[2]

While architects have a cultural aversion to seeing themselves as an increment of economic gain, they create value that they very often fail to record or capture. Until this value is expressed in a format that can be fed into policy and procurement, it will remain invisible and ignored, leaving economic value the sole dominant currency of built environment transactions. Though definitions may be limiting, they are necessary at this point in time to 'externalise' and make known the knowledge of architects.

Design value is widely accepted to be the sum of environmental, economic and social value,[3] in other words the commonly used 'triple bottom line' of sustainability. While environmental value is generally measured in embodied and operational carbon (sometimes with the addition of biodiversity), and there are existing practices (albeit flawed) for measuring economic value, there are no agreed measures of social value.

Flora Samuel and Eli Hatleskog, Design value constituents, 2018

The triple bottom line of sustainability. Architects need to be clear about types of value generated by architecture or run the risk of being ignored by decision-makers.

Defining Social Value

Geoffrey C Bowker and Susan Leigh Star note in their book *Sorting Things Out: Classification and Its Consequences* (1999) that orderings are always culturally and temporally specific and therefore need to be constantly under review. They call for a new form of information science that mixes 'formal and folk classifications'.[4] Such is the ordering that is posited here. Social value has much in common with 'resilience', which can be understood as a transformative condition that allows us not only to adapt, but also to transform and reinvent our society towards a more balanced, more equitable way of living on Earth.

It is difficult to say what social value is, but you know it when you see it. For the purposes of this ⌂, it is understood to relate to the wellbeing generated through the procurement of buildings and places, sometimes quantified. It has five overlapping dimensions. The first is the creation of jobs and apprenticeships, the version that has become a standard requirement of procurement in the UK and tends to be quite a blunt, tickbox-type exercise. Filling in the social value section in pre-qualification questionnaires (PQQs) and invitations-to-tender (ITTs) in the UK takes considerable expertise, experience and time, which is why larger organisations are often better at it, ironically excluding the smaller companies that social value legislation was designed to protect.

JOBS & APPRENTICESHIPS

WELLBEING GENERATED BY DESIGN

LEARNING DEVELOPED THROUGH CONSTRUCTION

DESIGNING WITH THE COMMUNITY

BUILDING WITH LOCAL MATERIALS

Social Value

Flora Samuel and Eli Hatleskog, The five overlapping dimensions of the social value of architecture, 2020

Architecture generates social value in multiple ways, but these are poorly understood.

It is important for construction teams to create jobs and training that deliver widespread long-term benefits to an area, both economic and social, as can be seen in Li Wan and Edward Ng's article on the benefits of utilising local technologies within village communities in China (pp 74–81). Similarly, Irena Bauman and Kerry Harker (pp 38–45) chart the development of Built InCommon, a network of neighbourhood-owned fabrication workshops designed to promote widespread innovation at a local scale. This is also a powerful theme in Doina Petrescu and Constantin Petcou's discussion of atelier d'architecture autogérée's R-Urban strategy (pp 30–37).

The second dimension of social value is the wellbeing generated by the design of a building or place – connecting inhabitants, promoting freedom and flexibility, encouraging positive emotions (for example, through exposure to nature) and meaningful engagement by allowing people a say in the design of their environments. The third dimension is the learning generated through construction. Jateen Lad's Sharanam project outside Pondicherry in India (pp 82–7) provides an exemplar of how communities can be involved in construction, acquiring new skills while creating a building that works well environmentally and facilitates contact with the natural environment.

Fourthly, there is social value in the learning that takes place when local people are involved in the design of their environment. Building a building should be a relationship, not an affair – an evocative metaphor delivered by the Grangetown community about a Community Asset Transfer bowls pavilion project in Cardiff, Wales, as discussed by Mhairi McVicar in her article (pp 46–51). It is not just about the building though; the real asset being transferred is the knowledge and confidence to make change, which is a two-way street between the community and the professional team.

As well as assisting with the design of their built structures, communities are increasingly also being involved in their construction. Building collectively was once traditional, and still is in some parts of the world. This empowering experience has been locked into the curriculum of architecture students at the University of Reading in Berkshire, UK. Their Urban Room, developed with Invisible Studio architects, was realised in 2019 and longlisted for the RIBA MacEwen Award for 'architecture for the common good'. Made as a temporary art venue, it was later dismantled and rebuilt in the grounds of a local primary school.

The last, much neglected dimension of social value is the benefit of building with local materials and typologies, and in doing so creating local jobs. Going against the grain of legislation and procurement, this is something that UK-based practice ADAM Architecture works hard to achieve, for example in their Nansledan ongoing extension to the town of Newquay in Cornwall.

What, then, is the appropriate response for an architect when a community values things other than architecture? This issue is problematised by Anthony Hoete in his article on the Māori *whare* (house) (pp 112–19), and is a conundrum faced by Mat Hinds in his contribution on the design of the Krakani lumi centre for eco-tourism in the cultural homelands of the palawa-pakana, the first peoples of lutruwita (Tasmania) (pp 120–27).

Capturing Social Value

The UK policy context is an exemplar of why social value is growing in traction in governments across the world. Since the advent of the Social Value Act 2012 and the Future Wellbeing of Generations (Wales) Act 2015, it has been gaining significance as a requirement of procurement, contracts and planning in the public sector.[5] Commonly expressed as the social value of the

As well as assisting with the design of their built structures, communities are increasingly also being involved in their construction

Invisible Studio,
Coppice Workers' Shelter,
Westonbirt Arboretum,
Tetbury, England,
2019

Making as connecting – empowering people and delivering new skills through the design and construction of simple structures.

Invisible Studio,
Urban Room,
School of Architecture,
University of Reading,
England,
2019

Co-designed and built with students
as a forum for conversation, the
project delivers multiple dimensions
of social value.

Building collectively was once traditional, and still is in some parts of the world. This empowering experience has been locked into the curriculum of architecture students at the University of Reading in Berkshire

ADAM Architecture,
Nansledan,
Newquay,
England,
2013-

Designed for the Duchy of Cornwall, this urban
extension scheme adds social value through the
use of local materials and details, but this takes
tenacity from both architect and client as it works
against the grain of current project delivery.

process and not the product, there is, however, growing consensus on the wellbeing impact of design and placemaking,[6] particularly now that 'social prescribing' is becoming such an integral part of National Health Service activity.[7] COVID-19 has brought the impact of places and the way they are designed into relief.

Organisations such as the Housing Associations' Charitable Trust (HACT) have been developing social value proxies for use by housing associations and local authorities to collect information on their portfolios, but as yet there are no mechanisms to capture the social value of design specifically, or to consider how it might be captured spatially. This is why independent research organisation Social Life's work on evaluating neighbourhood wellbeing, as discussed in Nicola Bacon and Paul Goodship's article (pp 60–67), is so significant.

The Social Value Toolkit for Architecture, developed bottom-up by the University of Reading with the London-based Research Practice Leads (RPL) group and published by the Royal Institute of British Architects (RIBA), is the first to offer architects a methodology for the monetisation of social value through the use of social return on investment (SROI), a technique that is gaining considerable traction across the UK and beyond.[8]

Post-occupancy evaluation (POE), returning to a building or place after it has been in use to find out how well it is performing, rarely happens, but is crucial for the measuring and mapping of intangible impacts such as social value, as well as the more tangible, for example energy performance. The boundaries between POE, conservation and history are blurred in Aoibheann Ní Mhearáin and Tara Kennedy's insightful study of St Brendan's, a 1960s community school in Ireland (pp 94–103). That the issue of scale is important can also be seen from Ayona Datta and Nabeela Ahmed's examination of gender safety and public infrastructure in the city of Thiruvananthapuram in India using participatory techniques as well as crowdsourced mapping to create a rich and inclusive account of women's experiences (pp 104–11).

New technologies, if used in an ethical and critical way, are set to make the capturing of social value much easier in the near future. There has been a surge of interest in data across research-led architecture practices in the last year. Jenni Montgomery's discussion of Greenkeeper, a pioneering digital platform that uses mobile phone data to monitor the usage of green space, provides an important illustration of a new type of innovation that is taking place in practice (pp 68–73). In her article, not only does Cristina Garduño Freeman chart social media traffic to measure the impact of the Sydney Opera House on Australia's identity, culture and economy, she also forensically captures the cumulative impact of stuff, the millions of fridge magnets, tea towels, bags and ephemera that celebrate its image across the globe (pp 88–93).

Why is Social Value Important?

Categorisation, the clustering of information, is the infrastructure of our 'built moral environment'.[9] Setting to one side the obvious ethical imperative to make buildings that are good for people (and by implication the planet), there are some important practical reasons to define and measure change in social value quantitively as well as qualitatively in an increasingly data-driven environment. We need to find ways to capture intangible impacts or they will not figure in future city models, BIM, parametric design, the assessment of project bids, the calculation of insurance premiums or outcomes-based building procurement in the delivery.[10] A multitude of tools are emerging within other disciplines to assist with this process, several of which are discussed in this issue, but it would be better if architecture could develop its own, to avoid becoming marginalised from the debate altogether. Leadership is urgently needed to communicate the role they play in generating social value in the built environment. ᗩ

New technologies, if used in an ethical and critical way, are set to make the capturing of social value much easier in the near future

Notes
1. Mariana Mazzucato, *The Value of Everything: Making and Taking in the Global Economy*, Allen Lane (London), 2018, p xix.
2. Geoffrey C Bowker and Susan Leigh Star, *Sorting Things Out: Classification and Its Consequences*, MIT Press (Cambridge, MA), 1999.
3. Bilge Serin *et al*, *Design Value at the Neighbourhood Scale*, UK Collaborative Centre for Housing Evidence, 19 November 2018: http://housingevidence.ac.uk/publications/design-value-at-the-neighbourhood-scale/.
4. Bowker and Leigh Star, op cit.
5. UK Green Building Council, *Driving Social Value in New Development: Options for Local Authorities*, 2019: www.ukgbc.org/wp-content/uploads/2019/03/UKGBC-Driving-social-value-in-new-development-Options-for-local-authorities-1.pdf.
6. Design Council and Social Change UK, *Healthy Placemaking*, April 2018: www.designcouncil.org.uk/sites/default/files/asset/document/Healthy_Placemaking_Report.pdf.
7. NHS England, *Healthy by Design: The Healthy New Towns Network Prospectus*, 2018: www.england.nhs.uk/wp-content/uploads/2018/01/healthy-by-design-healthy-new-towns-network-prospectus.pdf.
8. Flora Samuel *et al*, *Social Value Toolkit for Architecture*, Royal Institute of British Architects (London), 2020: www.architecture.com/knowledge-and-resources/resources-landing-page/social-value-toolkit.
9. Bowker and Leigh Star, *op cit*, p 32.
10. Flora Samuel, *Why Architects Matter: Evidencing and Communicating the Value of Architects*, Routledge (London), 2018.

DESIGN FOR IMPACT

Karen Kubey

WORKac, Kew Gardens Hills Library, Kew Gardens
Hills, Queens, New York, 2017

The Kew Gardens Hills Library came through the Department of Design and
Construction (DDC) Project Excellence programme and was designed as a
'vibrant social institution in a diverse community'. Project stakeholders set
goals according to the DDC's Project Excellence Design Value Survey, which
establishes design objectives in the categories of 'equity, healthy living,
sustainability, and resiliency'.

MEASURING ARCHITECTURE'S SOCIAL VALUE IN THE UNITED STATES

In a world where economic quantifiability seems to be paramount, urbanist **Karen Kubey**, a Faculty Fellow in Design for Spatial Justice at the University of Oregon, specialising in health and housing, examines how some US organisations are enhancing the case for participatory design, social impact and equitable urban design.

In the face of tight budgets and more easily quantifiable outcomes like the number of housing units produced, how can organisations make the case for the value of quality architecture and urban design, and for participatory design processes? Can these efforts shift ongoing patterns of inequitable investment in the built environment that short-change communities of colour and the poor? Though they use terms like 'social impact' and 'just design' instead of 'social value', the four examples below show US organisations and government agencies attempting to measure architecture's human benefits, comparing their strategies and systems of evaluation.

The Just City Index

Reflecting on her urban design and planning work in cities like Washington DC and Detroit, Toni L Griffin, founder of the Just City Lab research platform and Professor in Practice of Urban Planning at the Harvard Graduate School of Design (GSD), found that cities and funders were increasingly interested in measuring project and investment outcomes, but that their metrics were not addressing the racial and economic inequities she was observing on the ground: 'We were seeing a tremendous amount of *injustice*. We wanted to know whether design and planning can have an impact?'

Griffin started the Just City Lab in 2016, asking collaborators and the wider public to: 'Imagine a set of values that would define a community's aspiration for the Just City. Imagine we can assign metrics to measure design's impact on justice. Imagine we can use these findings to deploy interventions that minimize conditions of injustice.'[1] The Just City Index, the organisation's central measurement tool, is not a points system, but rather a framework that translates the concept of social justice into 50 'values indicators' that might appear in the built environment. These range from the more concrete 'Access: The convenient proximity to, quality of, or connectivity to basic needs, amenities, choices, and decisions', to the more abstract 'Delight: Creating places, spaces, and processes that promote happiness and joy'.

The Index is a purposively expansive tool, designed to allow communities to determine what would make their neighbourhood or city more just. 'Everyone says they want "equity," but no one defines it,' explained Griffin. 'What is equity, justice, and inclusion in Nairobi might be very different from Kansas City. This is not one-size fits all; we give you a *vocabulary* for you to construct it on your own. And those things change, too. We want it to be elastic, self-created, and connected to place.' She acknowledges that producing quality evaluative work is difficult: 'The challenge is that the things we want to measure are about inclusion; they can only be measured through qualitative measures, which means time and labour.' Her group is looking at the role of technology in measuring more qualitative user experience, to overcome the challenges of finding sufficient resources and time.

The Just City Lab,
Just City Index Values,
2017

right: The Just City Index is a framework intended to enable organisations, communities and civic leaders to develop a clear set of goals and intentions for addressing social and spatial justice in urban planning, design and development. Index values have been developed and tested through collaborative workshops around the world.

ACCEPTANCE Belonging · Empathy
Inclusion · Trust
Reconciliation
Respect · Tolerance

ASPIRATION Creative Innovation
Happiness
Hope · Delight
Inspiration

CHOICE Diversity
Spontaneity

DEMOCRACY Conflict
Debate
Protest
Voice

ENGAGEMENT Community
Cooperation
Participation
Togetherness

FAIRNESS Equality
Equity
Merit
Transparency

Authenticity
Beauty · Pride
Character
Spirituality · Vitality **IDENTITY**

Access
Connectivity **MOBILITY**

Accountability
Agency
Empowerment
Representation **POWER**

Adaptability
Durability
Sustainability **RESILIENCE**

Freedom
Knowledge
Ownership **RIGHTS**

Healthiness
Prosperity
Protection
Safety · Security **WELFARE**

DIVERSITY PUBLIC LIFE

J Max Bond Center in partnership with Gehl,
Public Life in New York City's Plazas,
New York,
2014

below: The J Max Bond Center on Design for the Just City at the Spitzer School of Architecture at the City College of New York, then headed by Toni Griffin, now of the Just City Lab, and deputy director Esther Yang, collaborated with Gehl to assess civic life and social justice in New York City public plazas, through an elaborate set of indicators and metrics. The study found more income diversity among plaza users than in surrounding neighbourhoods, but that the plaza users' racial makeup mirrored that of the adjacent area.

Plazas

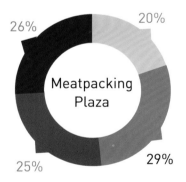

26% 20%
Meatpacking Plaza
25% 29%

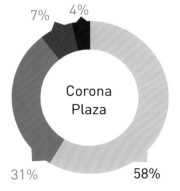

7% 4%
Corona Plaza
31% 58%

Neighborhoods

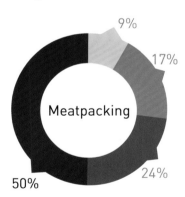

9% 17%
Meatpacking
50% 24%

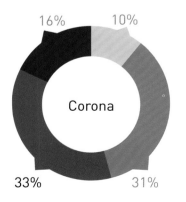

16% 10%
Corona
33% 31%

In focus: two extremes

Meatpacking

Corona Plaza

■ $0 - $14,999
■ $15,000 - $49,999
■ $50,000 - $99,999
■ $100,000 +

U.S. Census Bureau,
American Community
Survey 2009-2013, Five-year
estimates and Gehl/JMBC
Plaza Intercept Survey 2014

New York City Public Design Commission and Department of Design and Construction

Following New York City Mayor Bill de Blasio's 2014 mandate to fight the 'inequality that has created a "Tale of Two Cities" across the five boroughs',[2] City agencies are working to deliver quality architecture and urban design to neighbourhoods and communities that have seen decades of disinvestment. 'The narrative for a long time has been that whiter, wealthier communities got to have better design projects,' said Justin Garrett Moore, executive director of the Public Design Commission (PDC), the City's design review agency. 'We know that we can do better in communities that haven't had as much investment in the past.' Building on the Department of City Planning's Urban Design Principles, which advanced the idea that good urban design can promote social equity by being 'open and accessible to everyone',[3] the PDC developed Affordable Housing Guiding Principles[4] to set high standards for design in all neighbourhoods. The Commission, which has jurisdiction over permanent structures on City-owned property, including affordable housing built by private developers on land leased by the City, published the principles as it introduced a streamlined interagency design review process. Together, the principles and new process sought to engage the public and increase transparency in how the Commission assesses the social value of the designs that come before it.

Reporting to the Deputy Mayor for Housing and Economic Development, who is tasked with executing the City's plan to support the development or preservation of 300,000 affordable homes by 2026,[5] the PDC needs to communicate the value of quality architectural and urban design to officials and stakeholders concerned with production and cost. 'At the end of the day, it's like a translation service' between the fields of design, real-estate development and policy, explained Rebecca Macklis, the Commission's Senior Urban Design Manager. 'There might be a large policy initiative, but the built-scale, human-scale deliverable of that is a different thing.'

The New York City Department of Design and Construction (DDC), which manages the construction and renovation of public buildings like libraries and firehouses, advances social value in design through its Project Excellence programme, formerly known as Design and Construction Excellence. The programme uses quality-based selection to engage top architects and building professionals, rather than awarding contracts to the lowest bidder, and was established in 2004 as the first American municipal programme of its kind. 'We cannot assume that the term "excellence" is universally understood, so we look for opportunities to define it,' said Michaela Metcalfe, the department's Director of Project Excellence. Describing the ways that 'excellence' appears in the public spaces built through the programme, she says the spaces 'welcome and engage local history and culture, create a sense of community stewardship, provide vital resources, convey character and identity, lift the spirit and foster pride,

| 1. Site Planning | 2. Massing | 3. Materiality | 4. Facade |

New York City Public Design Commission (PDC), Guiding Principles for Quality Affordable Housing, New York, 2018

Ranging from site planning to building materials, the PDC's Guiding Principles codify ways in which affordable housing might be designed to benefit not only the City's residents, but also the wider public, including those visiting ground-floor retail or just walking by. The principles align with stages of the PDC's design review process; the City's Department of Housing Preservation and Development oversees interior design decisions, using its own guidelines.

BLA + WXY,
The Peninsula,
The Bronx, New York,
due for completion 2024

Planned for the site of the former Spofford Juvenile Detention Center in the South Bronx, The Peninsula is the first large-scale project to go through the Public Design Commission's streamlined design review process. Through the process, the mixed-use development, with 740 affordable apartments, commercial and light industrial, was redesigned to allow east–west pedestrian access through the site.

5.
Windows and Doors

6.
Ground Floor Condition

7.
Circulation

8.
Open Space Design

support diverse activities, provide opportunities for social exchange, encourage access, activity and movement, and support a sustainable, resilient, and healthy City for all'.

The DDC uses qualitative measures like its Project Excellence Design Value Survey to work with stakeholders to set design goals for a particular project, but does not have resources devoted to a 'scientific, data-driven process' of evaluation. Earlier tools translating post-occupancy survey responses into numbers seemed arbitrary and less useful to Metcalfe and her colleagues: 'There would have to be taxpayer money allocated to measuring. Are our communities interested in understanding the social value that way? Or maybe they understand the value inherently when a new library is built. Because we build for the public, we must be cognizant that the decisions we make every day – whether during design or construction – have an impact on the quality of life and resources available to the public.'

Social Economic Environmental Design (SEED)

A key figure in the US public-interest design movement, architect Bryan Bell co-founded the Social Economic Environmental Design (SEED) network to collect and promote examples of projects designed with and for marginalised communities. The framework was inspired by the US Green Building Council's LEED (Leadership in Energy and Environmental Design) programme, which measures a building's environmental impacts and has helped to raise the level of environmental sustainability of buildings in the US. Bell also wanted to provide a counterpoint to design projects that gain wide media attention without serving communities. 'It's easy to present a project as a success, when it could be an incredible failure' from the point of view of its users, he explained. 'How can we promote a measurement method as an empowerment tool for communities? We are validity seekers.'

To gain SEED certification for a project, an architect must define the key social, economic and environmental issues present, and then demonstrate how they worked with communities to meet the communities' goals in those areas. For Bell, and SEED, local participation in the design process is non-negotiable: 'In my opinion, "equity" means community ownership in a project. I don't see how you can create equity without valid participation.' That climate and economic crises put pressure on buildings to perform myriad social functions offers a critical role for architects: 'When we create value for society, society will pay us for it. That's the reason public health isn't going anywhere. Without it, we would die. Public health is only 70 years old. We're not there yet [as architects], but the end goal is demonstrating to society that value.'

Urban Design Build Studio (UDBS),
PROJECT RE_ Facility,
Pittsburgh, Pennsylvania,
2015

above: A Carnegie Mellon University UDBS student (left) and Trade Institute of Pittsburgh apprentice in training (right) work together to build an enclosure system made entirely of reclaimed building material and waste. The project's SEED certification identified 'social' objectives of Job Skill Development and Recidivism; the design and construction process fostered collaboration between people of divergent backgrounds.

below: Fulfilling the SEED 'environmental' goals of Design for Deconstruction, the prefabricated building components are designed to be able to be disassembled and reused for future alternative purposes. Created by students in the UDBS, this exploded perspective drawing illustrates the systems employed in the construction of the pavilions and entry canopy, demonstrating consideration of full life-cycle environmental impacts.

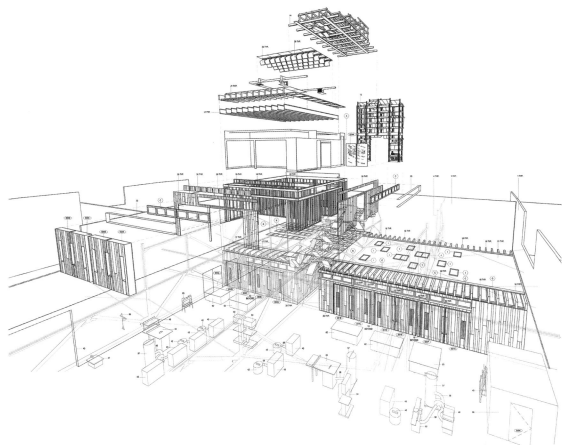

Enterprise Community Partners

Enterprise Community Partners, the national non-profit organisation that invests in affordable housing and provides technical assistance to local housing providers, pushes for social outcomes through tools like its Green Communities Criteria, a checklist of mandatory and optional features of the design process and resulting building, from designing for the health of the residents to locating housing near public transport, to specifying environmentally friendly materials. Twenty-six states either require or incentivise Green Communities certification as a condition of their affordable housing financing, giving Enterprise power to influence the characteristics of housing produced nationally.

Green Communities can be compared with the WELL Building Standard, a global rating system focusing more narrowly on buildings' contributions to human

Runberg Architecture Group,
The Marion West, Seattle,
Washington,
2016

Enterprise Community Partners influences the design of affordable housing countrywide through its Affordable Housing Design Leadership Institute, which brings together developers and architects to workshop the design of buildings like the 49-unit Marion West in the pre-development phase, and through its Green Communities Criteria, which have been used to certify affordable housing projects in 43 states and the District of Columbia. The Green Communities framework includes a series of mandatory and optional criteria towards the goals of environmental, economic and health outcomes for residents.

The measure of a structure or space's value must be grounded in the needs of the local people who use it

comfort, health and wellness. Administered since 2014 by the International WELL Building Institute, a public-benefit corporation, WELL measures and monitors human impact through the categories of air, water, nourishment, light, fitness, comfort and mind. In comparison, Enterprise's approach to evaluating affordable housing design is more holistic. 'We are creating tools to help designers and developers prioritise social outcomes. Our tools are about cultivating design leadership in people like executive directors [of community development corporations], who didn't know they were designers,' said Nella Young, the organisation's Senior Program Director in Design Leadership. Some of the design changes that might be made through Enterprise's tools are subtle, like a building's relationship to the street, but Young finds that a lot of developers are not focused on the ways that design can help meet their goals.

Recognising local developers' limited capacity for post-occupancy evaluation, Enterprise's mantra for its Design Matters tools was 'measuring less, but measuring it well'. The organisation invites developers to consider their project users' highest priorities, and implement measurable design decisions, for example, reducing preventable falls in senior housing: 'A lot of things you're measuring are proxies. Figuring out what you're going to measure and how to measure it is hard. That's why we say, "Just choose three".'

Valuing Human Outcomes

Going beyond economic return on investment, these examples consider how design can contribute to less quantifiable human outcomes, such as a sense of welcome or public ownership, particularly in low-income and minority neighbourhoods. Countering design media and prizes often focused on a building's image, they demand not only beauty, but also spaces that serve their communities. The measure of a structure or space's value must be grounded in the needs of the local people who use it. Against America's vast racial and economic inequities, these qualitative and quantitative approaches are tools in the fight for social justice. ∆

This article is based on separate phone interviews conducted by Karen Kubey in October and November 2019 with Toni L Griffin of the Just City Lab, Michaela Metcalfe of the New York City Department of Design and Construction, Justin Garrett Moore and Rebecca Macklis of the New York City Public Design Commission, Bryan Bell of the Social Economic Environmental Design (SEED) Network, and Nella Young of Enterprise Community Partners.

Notes
1. The Just City Lab: www.designforthejustcity.org/about.
2. New York City Office of the Mayor: www1.nyc.gov/office-of-the-mayor/bio.page.
3. New York City Department of City Planning, 'Urban Design Principles for Planning New York City': www1.nyc.gov/assets/planning/download/pdf/plans-studies/urban-design-principle/urban-design-principle-one-pager.pdf?r=3.
4. 'Affordable Housing Guiding Principles': www1.nyc.gov/assets/designcommission/downloads/pdf/5-8-2018_PDC_Affordable_Housing_Guiding_Principles.pdf.
5. 'Housing New York 2.0': www1.nyc.gov/assets/hpd/downloads/pdfs/about/housing-new-york-2-0.pdf.

Peter Andreas Sattrup

Vandkunsten,
Danmarkshusene,
Rødovre, Denmark,
2014

Keeping track of resources
when designing can improve
quality while lowering costs.
In Danmarkshusene, a social
housing project, rents were
22 per cent lower and carbon
emissions reduced by 68 per
cent compared to similar-scale
social housing. Occupants'
satisfaction was very high.

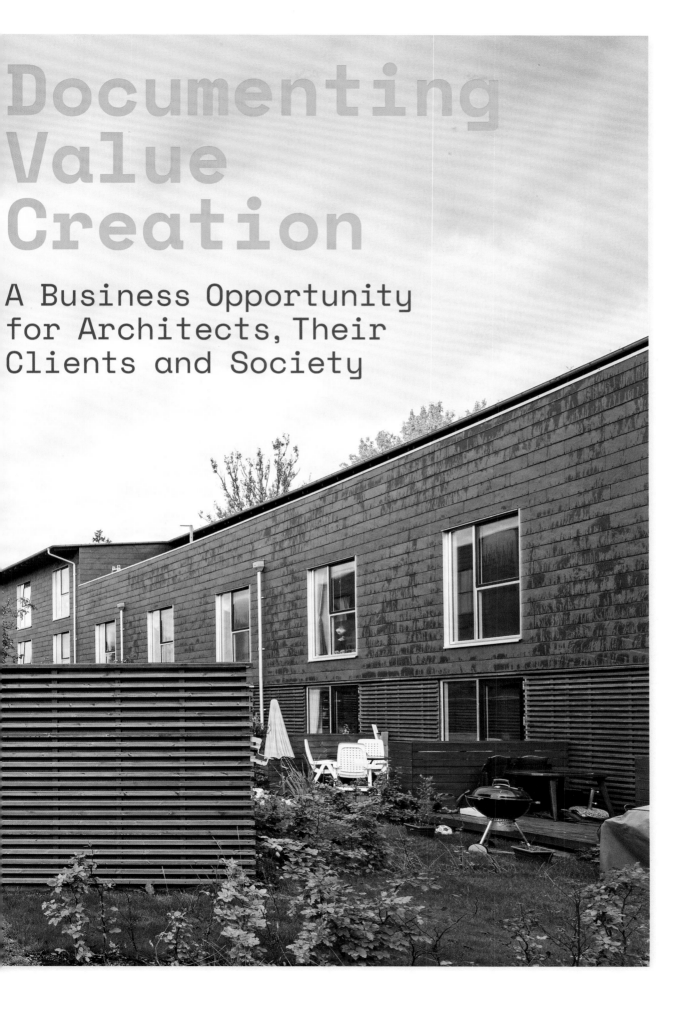

Documenting Value Creation

A Business Opportunity for Architects, Their Clients and Society

Architects have often neglected documenting the value of architectural design in terms their stakeholders understand, with detrimental effects on their fees and the esteem of their profession. But there are ways forward. Architect **Peter Andreas Sattrup**, Senior Advisor on Sustainability for the Danish Association of Architectural Firms, explains the association's framework for value creation by architectural design and how it can open up new business opportunities.

The Danish Association of Architectural Firms launched its Architecture Creates Value project in 2015, seeking to create a collection of case studies that could be used to communicate the impacts of architectural design, by pointing to well-documented realised projects that had been in use for some time. Members were invited to nominate and provide good cases of social, environmental and/or economic impacts of architectural design based on completed projects. Parallel to the call for case studies, a literature study was carried out. It found that there was generally quite limited research on the socioeconomic impacts of the built environment, and very little research that documented project-specific impacts. As it turned out, very few cases were adequately documented. Architects generally do not document the value they create in other terms than the architects' own accounts of design intentions and the project documentation by drawings, renderings and beautiful photographs. The built project itself seems to be understood as an implicit documentation of value.

Work was needed to define and explain how value is created by architectural design. Value is a relationship between benefits and costs, and is created through a collaborative effort involving many stakeholders in the construction value chain. Citing a 1998 Royal Academy of Engineering paper, Richard Saxon hypothesises that the total economic value created for the end users of a building may exceed the cost of development and construction by one or two orders of magnitude in a life-cycle perspective.[1] For its Architecture Creates Value project, the Danish Association of Architectural Firms wanted to document not just the economic value of architecture, but add social and environmental value dimensions as well, for a more comprehensive sustainability perspective. It was imperative to include these dimensions, as the social and economic benefits are typically enabled by the qualities of the built environment and at great cost to the natural environment, such as greenhouse gas emissions and habitat loss. But as these cost and benefit dimensions are rarely documented, they do not inform the financing models used by investors, to the detriment of the long-term quality of our environment and habitat.

Compelling Stories and Hard Facts
To qualify cases, a year was spent looking up documentation from all sorts of sources. It was mainly obtained from clients who had sponsored projects and who wanted to assess the social impacts of their investments, and from architects who either invested in research as part of their business strategy or worked consistently with documenting the sustainability performance of their projects. Architects' research was typically closely connected to some aspect of social, environmental or economic sustainability. Many cases had surprisingly powerful stories and impacts, covering virtually all aspects of life. Some architects had worked with methods from the social sciences, using post-occupancy evaluations to capture end users' experience

Peter Andreas Sattrup,
Value gearbox,
2019

Most value is created in the planning and design stages, at almost no cost compared to the life-cycle costs of construction, operation, maintenance and future adaptation of the building. The socioeconomic impacts on the building occupants are possibly on an entirely different order of magnitude but are almost never documented and therefore do not inform financing.

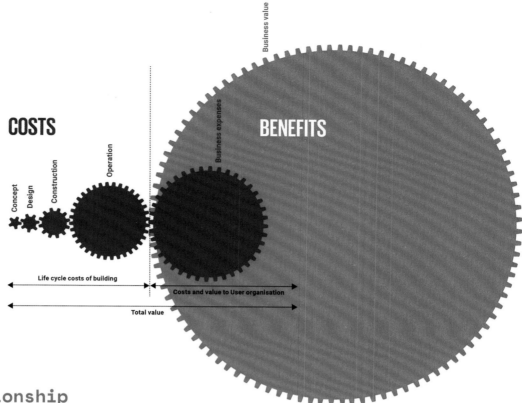

COSTS

BENEFITS

Concept
Design
Construction
Operation
Business expenses
Business value

Life cycle costs of building

Costs and value to User organisation

Total value

Value is a relationship between benefits and costs, and is created through a collaborative effort involving many stakeholders in the construction value chain

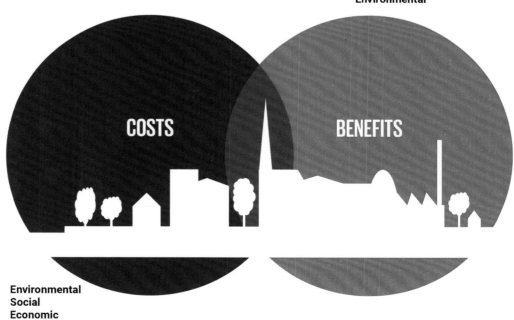

VALUE CREATION
**Economic
Social
Environmental**

COSTS

BENEFITS

Peter Andreas Sattrup,
Value creation and
resource management by
architectural design,
2019

Value can be defined as the relation between costs and benefits. Architecture suffers when its business models are based on short-term construction costs and immediate monetary gains: a lack of documented benefits leads to quality compromises. Value creation is redefined here in sustainability terms, on a long-term triple-bottom-line model.

**Environmental
Social
Economic**

RESOURCE MANAGEMENT

and use of spaces as indicators of social value. Others had worked with environmental engineering or economics. In some cases, the projects had enabled a marked change in user behaviour, which often was connected to economic value drivers.

The use of social science methods in Danish architecture is not new, as they were pioneered by Jan Gehl from the 1970s onwards and became the backbone of his urban design consultancy Gehl. In the case of New York City's Times Square, Gehl was asked in 2008 to improve traffic safety and did a comprehensive study of traffic patterns and urban life of the area as a premise for a temporary intervention: a large part of the square was closed off for cars, and street furniture was provided for pedestrians.[2] The intervention became an instant success with citizens and fuelled popular demand for a permanent solution which was implemented a decade later, designed by Snøhetta. Analysing usage patterns and social data, Gehl's input to reprogramming Times Square had radically transformed the quality and safety of the environment, considerably reducing traffic accidents and crime.

Other cases had been able to reduce environmental impacts and economic costs, while providing considerable social value. Danmarkshusene by Vandkunsten is a social housing project applying prefabricated modular construction techniques to pursue a philosophy of enabling tenants to operate and maintain the buildings and surrounding areas themselves. Vandkunsten use life-cycle costing (LCC) and life-cycle assessment (LCA) methods to keep track of long-term economic and environmental costs while they design. The results are impressive. Danmarkshusene has a 22 per cent lower rent and a 68 per cent lower carbon footprint than typical Danish social housing projects, and tenant satisfaction is very high.

The Danish Association of Architectural Firms published over 75 cases on www.danskeark.dk and an introductory booklet *Architecture Creates Value* in 2017.[3] The cases have many kinds of impacts that would be very interesting to research further, not least to be clearer about causalities, which are notoriously difficult to establish with precision. This is clearly an emerging field with a lot of research potential, and we are only at the very beginning of it. The collection of cases strengthened the Danish Association of Architectural Firms' communication and efforts to evidence the value of architecture. There are cases for almost any occasion when engaging political and economic stakeholders and the ordinary citizen. Quantifying the impacts of architecture is something that captures attention, particularly among political and economic decision-makers. The Architecture Creates Value project began to attract international attention too. There is great demand for knowledge of the performance of the built environment, and it is not limited to architects: many others – such as investors or representatives of user organisations – also naturally want to know how the built environment is an asset to them and their organisations, beyond property prices and rents.

Gehl,
Times Square intervention,
New York City,
2008

Jan Gehl was among the first to introduce social science methods to architectural practice almost half a century ago. His urban design consultancy Gehl's reprogramming of Times Square enabled a 40 per cent reduction in traffic accidents and a 20 per cent reduction in crime.

The intervention became an instant success with citizens and fuelled popular demand for a permanent solution which was implemented a decade later

There is major potential for innovation in the methods used for documentation. Patterns of connections between environmental qualities, social impacts and economic value were identified by looking across the many cases. Similarly, the methods used to document value were potentially applicable at all stages of a project from the ideation and initial design stages to the use stage and end of life. Clearly, the planning and design stages were where most value was created, but value could only truly be assessed by 'going back to the crime scene', as a Danish tongue-in-cheek expression has it. The Association's next move would be to empower architects to document the value created in their own projects.

A Methodology and DIY Guide to Value Creation

The Association spent another year 'connecting the dots' of how to create social, environmental and economic value and document it consistently. The aim was to establish a methodology that would be easy to communicate, easy to get started with, and easy to add further depth and complexity to, for anyone who was already an expert. The result was published in 2018. *ARCHITECT – Document Your Value Creation* is a framework and methodology for value creation that introduces a selection of methods to document the social, environmental and economic aspects.[4] All the methods are illustrated with cases, explaining how the methods were used in projects. The methodology is based on stakeholder dialogue, as the overarching question is: What values does architecture create, and for whom? A simplified three-step process is introduced, focusing on the initial planning and design stages where architects create most value, and on the use stage when a project has been operational for some time and values can be identified and measured. The simplification is important, as the intention is to inspire action among architects and investment from their clients in knowledge and better-informed processes, rather than scaring off practitioners with very demanding academic research standards. It is better to start researching in a simple yet consistent way than not to get started at all.

3XN,
Vandkunsten and Lendager,
Circle House,
Copenhagen, Denmark,
2018

Examples of facade cladding based on upcycled waste materials. Life-cycle assessments (LCA) and life-cycle costing (LCC) can be used to measure the resource efficiency of design solutions. This case documents that carbon emissions can be reduced by 40 to 60 per cent.

AART Architects,
VUC Syd,
Haderslev, Denmark,
2013

AART worked with anthropologists using post-occupancy evaluations to document the social value of selected projects. High satisfaction with the building's design qualities is linked to improved exam completion rates. Learning from users' positive and sometimes negative experience has improved AART's credibility with clients.

Peter Andreas Sattrup, Danish Association of Architectural Firms' methodology overview, 2019

Stakeholder dialogue forms the backbone of value creation. The fundamental question is mapping what values are created for which stakeholder groups, and how the values are designed for and experienced.

METHOD	PLAN	DESIGN	USE	INVESTORS
	Define stakeholders and chart their values, needs and preferences. Define **assignment**. Define **criteria** by which the success of the project can be assessed. Some criteria have to be measurable. Establish **Baseline**: Describe stakeholders' present conditions, activities and organisation, or use references for later comparisons.	Define which **design features** and process-related resources are to be used in the project in discussion with stakeholders. Assess and simulate the design's **qualities**. Assess what effects the solutions are expected to have, **adjust** the solutions if necessary.	**Evaluate** the qualities of the design with stakeholders. Measure **effects** in relation to success criteria. Include new criteria, where relevant. Document value creation by **comparing** measured and observed effects with the baseline and relating to costs.	USERS SOCIETY Map the value creation for these three groups of stakeholders.
SOCIAL	DEFINE SOCIAL OBJECTIVES	DESIGN FOR SOCIAL EFFECTS	DOCUMENT SOCIAL EFFECTS	INTERVIEWS OBSERVATION STUDIES QUESTIONNAIRES Document the social value creation.
ENVIRON-MENTAL	DEFINE ENVIRONMENTAL OBJECTIVES	DESIGN FOR ENVIRONMENTAL EFFECTS	DOCUMENT ENVIRONMENTAL EFFECTS	WELL-BEING AND HEALTH ENVIRONMENTAL QUALITIES LIFE CYCLE ASSESSMENT Document the environmental value creation.
ECONOMIC	DEFINE ECONOMIC OBJECTIVES	DESIGN FOR ECONOMIC EFFECTS	DOCUMENT ECONOMIC EFFECTS	CONSTRUCTION COSTS LIFE CYCLE COSTING TOTAL VALUE Document the financial value creation.

Value and Business Opportunities

A section of *ARCHITECT – Document Your Value Creation* let some of the pioneering architects explain how the methods are of value to themselves and their clients. According to the architects themselves, the methods generate a deeper knowledge of the impacts of planning and design on user behaviour and the impacts of the built environment when used properly. The resulting new knowledge is seen as a very important benefit of the research, because knowledge is fundamentally what architects sell. Having consistent methods for documenting impacts and value is argued to improve the credibility of architects as consultants, and for the individual office the competencies and services developed from the research are seen to offer significant competitive edge.

At present the Danish Association of Architectural Firms is sharing the findings and assisting its member companies in implementing them in their strategic business development and applying them in projects with their clients. The aim is to build a market for the research services by communicating opportunities to investors and political decision-makers in Denmark as well as internationally. The Association is also very keen to share findings with colleagues internationally, as architects everywhere seem to struggle for recognition and relevance in the eyes of political and economic decision-makers.

Contributing to Sustainable Development Goals

The next stage will seek to create international partnerships to connect value creation to the United Nations' 17 Sustainable Development Goals (SDGs). There is a pressing need to improve the quality of the built environment while dramatically reducing resource use and negative environmental impacts. As architecture and the SDGs are the theme of the upcoming International Union of Architects (UIA) 2023 World Congress of Architects to be held in Copenhagen,[5] the Danish Association of Architectural Firms plans to frame value creation in terms of the SDGs, to enable architects to document and communicate their contributions towards a sustainable built environment. ⌂

Notes

1. Richard Saxon, *Be Valuable: A Guide to Creating Value in the Built Environment*, 2005, p 26 ff: www.saxoncbe.com/be-valuable.pdf – citing Raymond Evans, Richard Haryott, Norman Haste and Alan Jones, *The Long-Term Cost of Owning and Using Buildings*, Royal Academy of Engineering (London), 1998.
2. New York City Department of Traffic, *World Class Streets: Remaking New York City's Public Realm*, 2008, http://www.nyc.gov/html/dot/downloads/pdf/World_Class_Streets_Gehl_08.pdf
3. www.danskeark.dk/en/content/architecture-creates-value.
4. www.danskeark.dk. Originally published in Danish as A*RKITEKT – dokumenter din værdiskabelse*: www.danskeark.dk/content/arkitekt-dokumenter-din-vaerdiskabelse-1.
5. https://uia2023cph.org/.

Henning Larsen Architects, Frederiksbjerg Skole, Aarhus, Denmark, 2016

HLA have developed a sustainability engineering department that works closely with designers. Recent developments link environmental qualities that can be modelled by design teams to social and economic impacts.

RESILIENCE VALUE IN THE FACE OF CLIMATE CHANGE

Doina Petrescu and Constantin Petcou

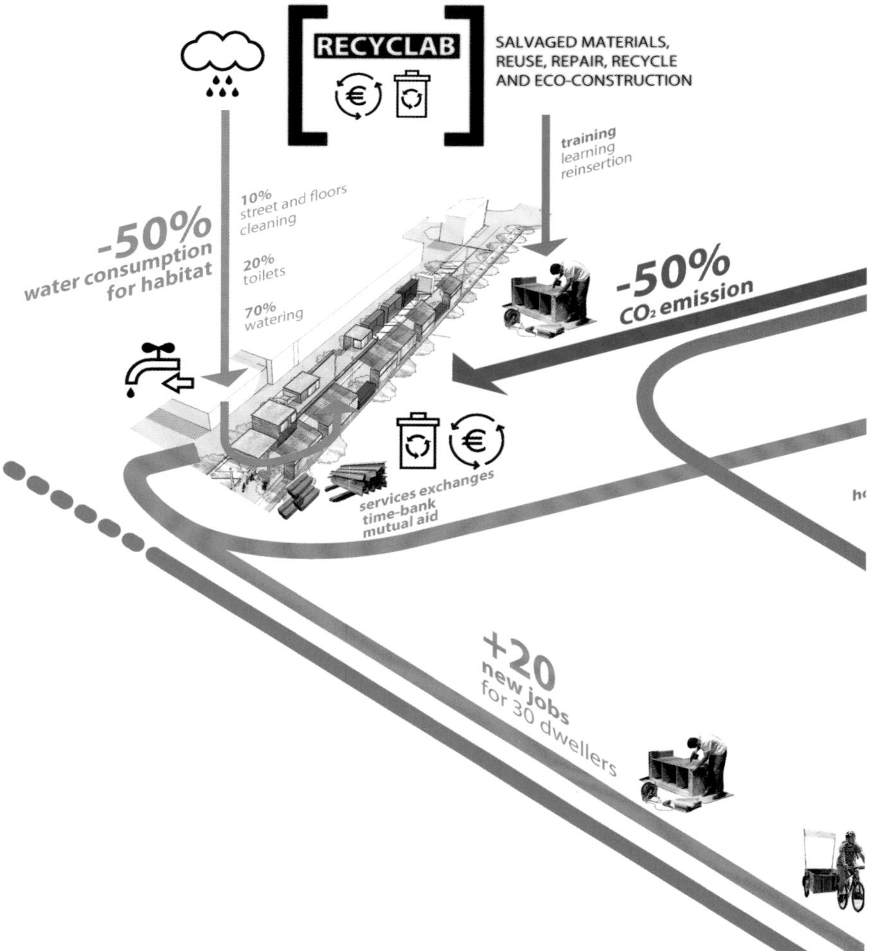

RECYCLAB

SALVAGED MATERIALS,
REUSE, REPAIR, RECYCLE
AND ECO-CONSTRUCTION

training
learning
reinsertion

-50%
water consumption
for habitat

10%
street and floors
cleaning

20%
toilets

70%
watering

-50%
CO_2 emission

services exchanges
time-bank
mutual aid

+20
new jobs
for 30 dwellers

atelier d'architecture autogérée,
Pilot units and ecological cycles,
The R-Urban network,
Colombes, Paris,
2011

The diagram shows the network of three resilience
hubs in Colombes functioning through locally
closed circuits and creating social, economic and
ecological benefits.

How can architecture enable civic ecological practices and community economies to fight climate change? **Doina Petrescu and Constantin Petcou,** founding members of Paris-based atelier d'architecture autogérée, describe strategies that have been developed to facilitate this virtuous resilience cycle particularly in relation to their project R-Urban.

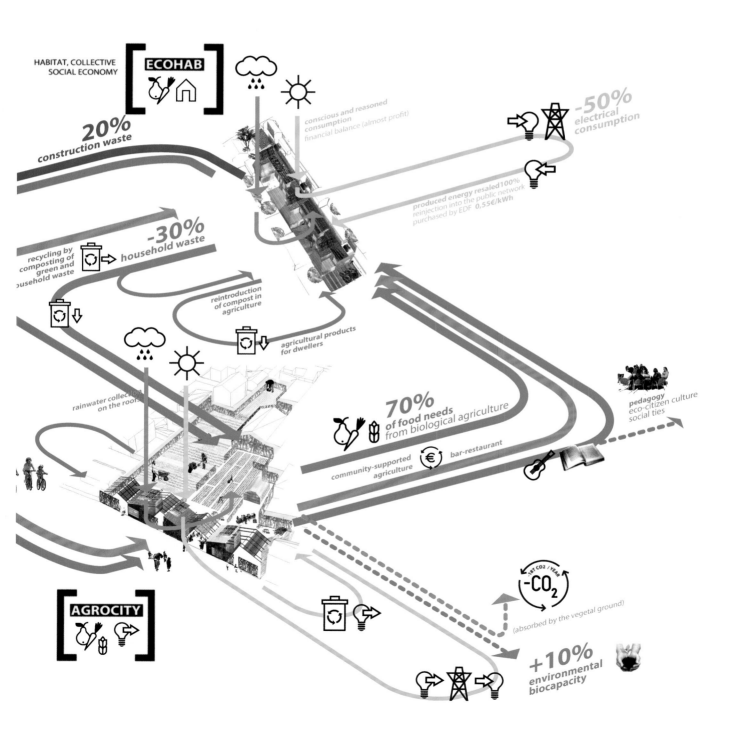

HABITAT, COLLECTIVE SOCIAL ECONOMY

ECOHAB

20% construction waste

-50% electrical consumption

conscious and reasoned consumption financial balance (almost profit)

produced energy resaled100% reinjection into the public network purchased by EDF **0,55€/kWh**

recycling by composting of green and household waste

-30% household waste

reintroduction of compost in agriculture

agricultural products for dwellers

rainwater collection on the roofs

70% of food needs from biological agriculture

pedagogy eco-citizen culture social ties

community-supported agriculture

bar-restaurant

AGROCITY

$-CO_2$

(absorbed by the vegetal ground)

+10% environmental biocapacity

R-Urban is a participatory strategy initiated by atelier d'architecture autogérée (aaa), based on the setting up of interconnected self-managed collective hubs, which boost the capacity of resilience within neighbourhoods by providing spaces where skills, knowledge, labour and creativity around urban agriculture, recycling, eco-construction and cooperative housing are shared.[1] As such, the R-Urban model proposes a resilient alternative to the current way of governing resources within a community and beyond. The 'R' of R-Urban stands for 'resilience' understood as 'resourcefulness', situating resilience in a positive light and relating it to the empowerment and agency of citizens and emergent communities. Although initially conceived by architectural designers and urban researchers, the R-Urban framework is further co-implemented with a wide range of actors including local residents, policy-makers and businesses.

The hubs and their local ecological systems constitute a form of urban infrastructure that can contribute to a wider ecological transition in neighbourhoods rooted in new collaborative social and economic practices. They act as prototypes for new ways of building and managing the neighbourhood and demonstrate the positive impacts of ecological transition, generating economic, ecological and social benefits.

The strategy was implemented from 2011 in Colombes, a suburban town to the northwest of Paris, in partnership with the municipality and a number of local organisations. Three hubs were planned to be built there – Agrocité, Ecohab and Recyclab – each aiming to provide complementary facilities (respectively urban agriculture and local culture, cooperative ecological housing, and recycling and eco-construction), enabling citizen-run services and local economic and ecological systems. In the event only two were built: Agrocité and Recyclab. They were operational in Colombes for five years before being relocated by aaa to two other neighbouring towns – Gennevilliers and Nanterre – because of a change of the municipal team following local elections.

With a reactivated local community, a number of ecological parameters were directly improved through the way in which the hubs were conceived and functioned. Food was produced locally; rainwater was collected and grey water remediated and used for watering; and urban waste was collected and transformed within the hubs. The numerous social and ecological benefits that they brought about included annual reductions of 37.3 tonnes in CO_2 emissions (ie 142 per cent less than traditional buildings of similar size and programme), 330 tonnes in waste, 24,500 cubic metres (865,000 cubic feet) in water consumption and an overall 40 per cent of the ecological footprint, with 50 per cent of the energy necessary for their functioning being produced locally.[2]

Given that the whole activity of R-Urban is oriented towards increasing resilience in the neighbourhood, all these benefits constitute a 'resilience value'. The questions here are: How can this value be assessed?

What components of the architectural project contribute to it? And how can the value of resilience be made an important parameter in architectural and urban projects?

Calculating Resilience Value
To answer these questions, research conducted together with economists Katherine Gibson and Maliha Safri from the Community Economies Collective (CEC) has put forward a method of calculating the value created by the R-Urban project in a way that also captures its collective resilience value.[3] Currently, the tools available to assess the value of any urban or architectural project are based exclusively on financial calculations. However, in a world where the aim is to promote ecologically sustainable development, the value question needs to go beyond financial capital and commodification to include nurturance and eco-maintenance. Determining full benefit requires identifying improvements in household, community and ecological health, social and psychological wellbeing, civic involvement and participatory democracy.

In *Take Back the Economy: An Ethical Guide for Transforming Our Communities*, JK Gibson-Graham (the feminist economists Katherine Gibson and Julia Graham), Jenny Cameron and Stephen Healy proposed a different tool which is the community economy return on investment (CEROI).[4] A community economy is built upon ethical investments – in surviving well, distributing surplus, responsibly encountering others, consuming sustainably and sharing our planetary resources, all with a view to the wellbeing of future more-than-human generations. Community economy returns thus include both social benefits (such as increased forms of individual, household and community wellbeing) and ecological benefits (such as a reduced ecological footprint and ecological repair). They also include increased collectively controlled surplus, increased ethical trade and expanded commons.

In a diverse economy that recognises the contributions of both paid and unpaid labour – including volunteer work, caring work and governance work, to name just a few – monetary equivalents can be used to 'cost' labour, products and services that are not exchanged via the market and are not 'commodified'.

Given the pertinence of the CEROI tool for the case of R-Urban, it is used here as a guide to calculate the full benefits of the strategy. A matrix has thus been established to measure four distinct aspects of the hubs: the direct financial revenues generated for individuals and the collective; the value of unpaid labour; the value of increased individual capacities; and the cost savings to users' households, the state and the planet.

The first aspect – the direct financial revenues – include design and research commission revenues related to new R-Urban developments, and the selling of services and goods produced by the R-Urban hubs (ie vegetables, cafe meals, fees for the different training courses: compost, apiculture, permaculture, etc).

The second – the value of unpaid labour related to R-Urban – is estimated by referring to the market value of each particular form of labour. A large amount of unpaid architectural and construction labour was volunteered by users to complete the design and construction work done by professionals and add further features in order to appropriate the project and adapt it to needs. Another large bulk of volunteering work concerned the growing and processing of food, both for sale and for direct use in the cafe. Volunteer contributions were also made by researchers, scientists, trainers, etc. A significant amount of volunteer hours were put into event organising, managing group activities, administering the hubs and book-keeping for hubs governance.

The third aspect includes the value of the new capacities and skills that participants gained by involvement in the broad range of R-Urban activities, including regular gardening and care, recycling and repair activities, workshops around particular skills, and ecological and cultural events such as conferences, symposia, seminars and art exhibitions.

Lastly, the saved costs to users' households, the state and the planet include the value of ecological repair such as CO_2 emissions reduction, air pollution reduction, increased biodiversity, waste collection and transformation, and green energy production. The ecological principles considered in the design of the R-Urban infrastructure meant that there were savings in building costs, energy and water use. Also R-Urban participants learnt new habits of reducing water consumption and carried them through into their household management and everyday life. The state saved social benefits for those people who have taken training in the R-Urban hubs and gained employment. Also participation in physical and social activities reduced health costs to households and the state. Adopting reusing, repairing and recycling of used goods in the function of the hubs and through barter and exchange schemes generated savings for individual participants.

atelier d'architecture autogérée,
Architecture and construction
activities at the Agrocité hub,
Gennevilliers, Paris,
2017

Dismantling and reconstruction in Gennevilliers of the Agrocité hub formerly located in Colombes. Ninety per cent of the materials initially used in Colombes were recovered and reused in the reconstruction process.

The ecological principles considered in the design of the R-Urban infrastructure meant that there were savings in building costs, energy and water use

atelier d'architecture autogérée,
Culture, research and pedagogy
activities at the Agrocité hub,
Colombes, Paris,
2013

Training workshop conducted by Professor Fionn Stevenson from Sheffield University with Agrocité users to work on R-Urban ecological circuits.

atelier d'architecture autogérée,
Economic activities at the Agrocité hub,
Colombes, Paris,
2014

Collective catering during public events was one of the diverse economic activities based on voluntary work developed at Agrocité. The monetary revenues of these activities were further collectively reinvested in other R-Urban activities.

atelier d'architecture autogérée, Environmental care activities at the Agrocité hub, Colombes, Paris, 2014

Self-organised bicycle repair sessions took place regularly in the Agrocité greenhouse, as one of the many environmental care activities.

atelier d'architecture autogérée, Wellbeing activities at the Agrocité hub, Colombes, Paris, 2015

The architecture of Agrocité allowed a diversity of activities to take place in parallel and encouraged encounters and exchanges between participants. This constructed and supported conviviality contributed to the increased wellbeing of the hub's users.

atelier d'architecture autogérée, Ecological prototypes at the Agrocité hub, Colombes, Paris, 2013

The rainwater collector storing 20 cubic metres (700 cubic feet) of water in the basement of Agrocité is one of the prototyped devices supporting ecological practices such as reduced water consumption in garden watering.

These returns were grouped according to the different areas of activity of the project. They comprised: culture, research and pedagogy (including activities of research, training, and education); architecture and construction (including design of the hubs and related devices, building of furniture and ecological devices for R-Urban hubs and external clients, DIY, recycling, repairing activities); economy (including small business and job training activities such as farming, catering, compost making, beekeeping, repairing etc); wellbeing (including individual and social wellbeing, reduced delinquency, reduced consumption, health improvements etc); ecology (including gardening, repair, reuse and other ecological care activities and their consequences on the environment); and management, care and governance (including activities such as repairing, cleaning, bookkeeping, communication, events organisation etc).

All these returns were estimated in monetary terms in order to speak about the broader social and environmental value of R-Urban (and other similar projects) in a 'language' that can be understood by policy-makers and urban developers. The method allows this specific resilience regeneration project to be compared with other urban development projects, and enables a post-capitalist vision and politics to be supported here and now.

Data were collected annually over a five-year period (2011 to 2016). Only the graphic representations of final data, and not the details of the calculations, are given in this article.[5] This exercise can be continued for subsequent iterations of R-Urban hubs, and provides a calculation and graphic representation guide for other similar projects.

The Resilience Value Iceberg

The value of the R-Urban project's social and ecological benefits, as estimated here, is something that is invisible most of the time, and is not generally included in any type of value calculation for urban projects. However, for a community-oriented project it is exactly this value which makes the difference.

This difference is evidenced by a graphic representation of data that recalls JK Gibson-Graham's iceberg model of the economy, first published in 2006 in *Postcapitalist Politics*.[6] For Gibson-Graham:

The image of the economy as an iceberg is one way of reframing which practices are included and valued as 'economic'. When we see the whole iceberg above and below the waterline, the economy as we have known it melts away. We start to recognize the vast range of practices, places, organizations and relationships that contribute to daily survival. What was once seen as 'alternative' is but part of the already existing diverse economy.[7]

Gibson-Graham speak also about the need to recognise the enabling aspect of the built environment in terms of allowing these 'diverse economies' that promote collectivity and sharing, or allowing care to be enacted. R-Urban is indeed an exemplary case of how an architectural project can create specific spaces to enable

JK Gibson—Graham,
The Economy as an Iceberg,
2013

Economic geographers Katherine Gibson and Julia Graham (aka JK Gibson-Graham) created the image of the iceberg of diverse economies, which was redrawn by artist James Langdon for the 'Trade Show' curated by Kathrin Böhm and Gavin Wade at Eastside Projects, Birmingham, in 2013–14. A group exhibition, the show exercised the function of art to exchange, present and enact different economic practices and cultures of trade.

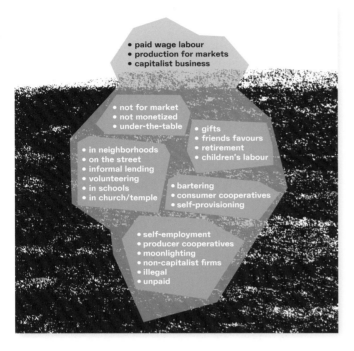

atelier d'architecture autogérée,
The 'iceberg' diagram of resilience value for R—Urban,
Colombes, Paris,
2011—16

below: The diagram shows the evolution of the resilience value produced by the R-Urban project during its five-year installation in Colombes, represented by the evolution of its 'economy' iceberg. Additional detail is shown in a one-year snapshot (2016).

collectivity, sharing and care and promote social and ecological values.

By analogy with Gibson-Graham's iceberg, the R-Urban resilience value diagram draws a hypothetical waterline which separates the visible and invisible parts of the value iceberg. The visible part represents the direct financial revenues generated by the project (ie the revenues from selling of services and goods produced by participants in the R-Urban hubs). This represents the part of the R-Urban economy which relates to the market. The invisible part monetises savings from voluntary work and skill improvements, as well as ecological savings generated during the construction and utilisation of buildings and through the activities they host. This is the plural and diverse economy of the project which is social and ecological. It also includes the 'enabling' value of the architecture which makes collectivity, or sharing, possible, or allows care to be enacted to save social costs for the state or ecological costs for the planet.

The calculations show that for an apportioned annual investment of €250,000 during the five-year period (including the costs of building and management of the two hubs), the yearly return on investment (which includes the value of ecological and environmental repair embedded in the hub's activities) grows gradually over time, reaching almost €2 million in 2016.

Looking at the evolution of the iceberg, it is noticeable that it is mainly the invisible value which grows exponentially. As such, in the fifth year (2016) the invisible value is 10 times larger than the visible market value. While the market value is created by only a few businesses incubated by the R-Urban hubs and involving tens of people, the invisible value is collectively created by hundreds of participants. The more participants join the project, the larger the generated invisible value is. As such, the wellbeing value increases because more people reduce their consumption and health costs, while increasing their sociality, skills and capacities.

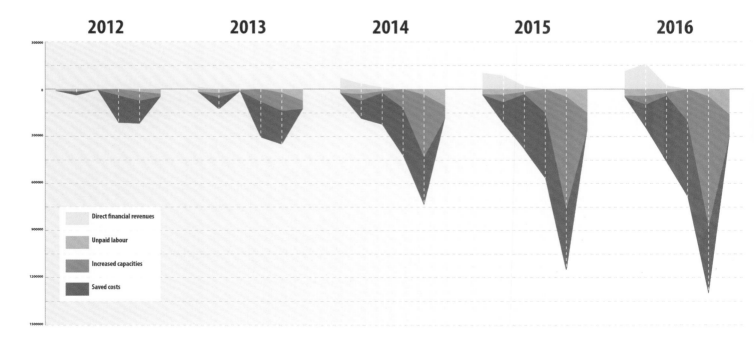

The savings for the state and the planet also increase as more people join the project to achieve ecological repair, being involved in activities of recycling and reducing of waste or in gardening, with consequences including a reduction of CO_2 emissions and air pollution and an increase in biodiversity.

The most significant increase is in the field of wellbeing and ecology, in terms of the estimated value of increased capacities and saved costs. However, this value is never considered in current transactions, and projects like R-Urban are usually dismissed because they do not generate direct financial value in the way a developer project does. This was the case with two of the R-Urban hubs which were threatened with eviction in 2016 by the then Mayor of Colombes, who wanted to sell and develop their sites on a capitalist model, for financial profit, dismissing the social, cultural and ecological values created by these hubs. In fact, nothing is wrong with these hubs; what is wrong is the power system which assesses the values they create.

The calculations demonstrate that these types of project generate even more important sorts of value: savings for the state and for the planet, as well as added social value and increased wellbeing. These value types can contribute very directly to covering the costs involved in the ecological transition. This is the 'resilience value', and is something that should be considered an integral part of the diverse economy-ecology of any architectural or urban project.

Lessons Learned on How to Act Against the Climate Crisis

R-Urban offers insight into how architecture can help to radically transform everyday practices and strengthen urban resilience. The setting up of community infrastructure where learning and exchange can take place alongside the activities of gardening, recycling and repair activities is important. Space is required for people to learn how to participate in community economy transactions and negotiations. The design and architectural qualities of R-Urban contribute to this. Without designated spaces for convivial exchange during winter, or places to hang out and make food together, the connections and trust building necessary to develop these practices are harder to make and sustain. Also, specific conditions are necessary to allow the project to grow its activities and its number of users over time. The R-Urban experience suggests this as a rule for increasing the invisible part of the resilience value iceberg. In addition, R-Urban's resilience value demonstrates that society actually has the means to act effectively against the climate crisis if opportunities are created for everyone to invest in and collectively reconsider the economic, social and ecological values of their actions. ⌂

2016

Notes
1. See the project website: http://R-Urban.net.
2. Doina Petrescu, Constantin Petcou and Corelia Baibarac, 'Co-producing Commons-Based Resilience: Lessons from R-Urban', *Building Research & Information*, 44 (7), 2016, p 729.
3. Doina Petrescu, Constantin Petcou, Katherine Gibson and Maliha Safri, 'Calculating the Value of the Commons: Generating Resilient Urban Futures', in *Transformative Geographies of Community Initiatives* profile issue of *Environmental Policy and Governance*, 2020 (in press).
4. JK Gibson-Graham, Jenny Cameron and Stephen Healy, *Take Back the Economy: An Ethical Guide for Transforming Our Communities*, University of Minnesota Press (Minneapolis), 2013.
5. http://R-Urban.net.
6. JK Gibson-Graham, *Postcapitalist Politics*, University of Minnesota Press (Minneapolis), 2006.
7. JK Gibson-Graham, *Economic Meltdown, or What An Iceberg Can Tell Us About The Economy*, Trade Show Eastside Projects (Birmingham), 2013, p 1.

Irena Bauman
and
Kerry Harker

New Infrastructure for Communities Who Want to Build

Does the concentration of production of prefabricated housing elements have a negative impact on communities? Would localised fabrication facilities enhance social value in self-build housing areas? Architect **Irena Bauman** and curator **Kerry Harker** explain their approach to and development of the Built InCommon methodology for local digital fabrication clusters.

Matt Murphy,
MassBespoke Flying Factory,
2018

The full factory setup costs approximately £100,000 (at 2019 prices) and is delivered to site in two steel containers. It can be shared by many community development trusts or used for training. The equipment and the containers can also be rented to allow for the Flying Factory to be disassembled when no longer needed.

Much has been written over the last few years about social value, wellbeing and happiness. As the popular understanding of the extent of the damage bestowed on society by greed, xenophobia and vanity is growing with every story of economic, social and environmental injustice, economists have begun to consider how to measure aspects of successful societies. Typically, national financial measures, such as gross domestic product (GDP) and gross national product (GNP), have been used as a measure of success. Although there are associations between GDP and individual happiness, with people in wealthier nations being happier than those in poorer nations, there is also evidence that happiness does not increase significantly once basic needs and security of comfort are achieved. Furthermore, society as a whole is happier when discrepancies of wealth are less pronounced. Kate Pickett and Richard Wilkinson, co-founders of the British charity The Equality Trust, have substantiated this link in their book *The Spirit Level*[1] and further maintain that inequality diminishes social life: 'What we value most is laughing, joking, relaxing and spending time with friends and family. That is essential to health and happiness – and yet it's there that inequality strikes.'[2]

Notions of wellbeing and happiness are being embraced as valuable, and new measures and indices are being developed to quantify such benefits. One of these is social value, a way of quantifying the relative importance of impacts that are not already captured in financial or market transactions. This article focuses on Built InCommon – a system for the generation of social and environmental value using digital technologies for self-build housing, developed as a dialogue between Bauman Lyons Architects and an arts organisation, East Leeds Project.

A Network of Neighbourhood-Owned Factories

The real benefit of new digital technologies in the built environment lies in a different, disruptive business model of a distributed network of small-scale, localised fabrication workshops with resilient ownership models. If the construction industry is to step up to the plate in harnessing digital technologies, it also needs to encourage disruptors into the market who have a different vision of a new economy for a just and sustainable society. One such disruptive idea was developed over the last two years by Bauman Lyons Architects (BLA) and their startup fabrication company MassBespoke.

BLA proposed a Built InCommon[3] network of neighbourhood-based/ collectively owned factories where goods and buildings are manufactured by local makers. The Built InCommon concept builds on the evolution of a booming community-led housing sector, and the emergence of digital construction systems such as WikiHouse, a timber-frame open-source system, and MassBespoke, a timber-cassette parametrically integrated construction method developed by BLA. These systems are designed to be fabricated using affordable digital tools such as computer-numerically controlled (CNC) routers that can be accommodated in small, local workshops. Together these trends can disrupt the current procurement of housing. They propose to exchange the development profits extracted by private developers for social value generated and retained locally.

There can be as many variations of Built InCommon business models as there are place-specific projects. However, all are community-owned assets, and there are three broad categories within which these models are embedded: a temporary facility set up for a specific project; expansion of an existing workshop to secure a more reliable order book and the smoothing out of peaks and troughs in workloads; and a new purpose-built workshop. Built InCommon factories offer direct opportunities to build good housing, workplaces and civic buildings by engaging local supply chains and those in the community with skills and a desire to build. This creates local training opportunities and stimulates local business. It also delivers on the social value indicators of creating positive emotions, connecting people, and offering freedom and flexibility in design-and-build community assets. The generation of social value is prioritised over private profit in the Built InCommon process. Work on exploring the potential of mapping social value within this process is in its very early stages but visualising the social impact of construction processes has the potential of evidencing the benefits of embedding social impact thinking in the procurement process.

The Ecology of Built InCommon

Built InCommon aims to challenge the negative social impact of centralised fabrication of buildings by creating opportunities for positive changes in people's lives through participation in the development and construction process. In order to embed social value impact thinking into the process of construction, BLA are working with several community activists to initiate development of strategies for increasing social value for their built projects. BLA are forming the strategy by using the four stages set out by Social Value UK in their *Maximise Your Impact* toolkit.[4]

MassBespoke,
Blok CNC workshop,
Hull, England,
2019

MassBespoke is a new-generation digital construction system suitable for small-scale, distributed digital fabrication. Here, sample MassBespoke cassettes are fabricated and assembled during a workshop at Blok CNC in Hull.

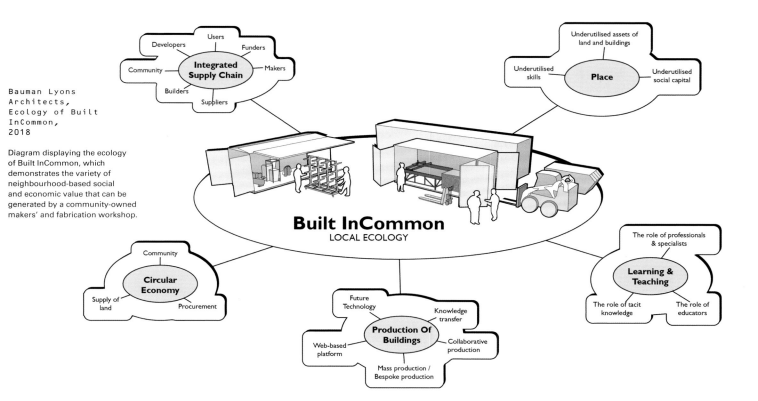

Bauman Lyons
Architects,
Ecology of Built
InCommon,
2018

Diagram displaying the ecology of Built InCommon, which demonstrates the variety of neighbourhood-based social and economic value that can be generated by a community-owned makers' and fabrication workshop.

In stage one, 'Plan', the project team have planned the project including identifying the organisations and the individuals to engage and set targets for the maximum social value impact that the projects hope to achieve. Stage two, called 'Do', is about to commence with delivery of the makers' space project. The project team will be collecting quantitative data to measure the targeted social value impact as the project is implemented. In stage three, 'Assess', the team will analyse the data to compare the outcomes against planned targets and to gain greater understanding of what is valued by various shareholders. In the final stage, 'Revise', the findings from the analysis will generate a set of recommendations for how the Built InCommon facility can be improved to generate higher social value and how the model can be scaled up. BLA are introducing mapping into the planning stage, hoping to continue developing this as a tool for visualising social impact and making it more tangible than numbers alone could ever do.

The Art of Building Communities
The East Leeds Project (ELP) is an arts organisation based within the local authority ward of Gipton & Harehills in the English city's eastern suburbs where its directors, Kerry Harker and Claire

Bauman Lyons Architects,
East Leeds Pavilion,
Leeds, England,
2019

Stage one – the 'Plan' stage of social value mapping – shows the existing organisations in East Leeds who were already generating social value for the area and could be potential partners for the East Leeds Pavilion makers' space project.

Irving, have lived for over 20 years. All but one of the 'lower-layer super output areas' (LSOAs) rank in the top 10 per cent most deprived in the country, based on 2019 Indices of Multiple Deprivation data.[5]

Attempting to generate new cultural infrastructure within this environment presents the ELP with multiple challenges. In contrast to the city centre and more affluent suburbs, cultural infrastructure is sparse and the formal spaces of museums and galleries, theatres, cinemas and music venues are all but entirely absent. In addition, the post-industrial spaces traditionally favoured and repurposed by artists and self-organised, small-scale arts initiatives are missing from a topography that was characterised until relatively recently by open farmland. Even the empty retail spaces which have given rise to the recent wave of 'pop-up' arts spaces within city centres, often criticised for their complicity with processes of 'creative place-making', as they serve only to enhance the economic value of private property, are not to be found here. New strategies are essential, and as a result the arts initiatives working locally have gravitated towards alternative spaces sited amid east Leeds's dense residential mass, including a decommissioned fire station and a deconsecrated Methodist chapel.

The ELP's approach is a form of social practice, defined as 'a collaborative, collective, and participatory social method for bringing about real-world instances of progressive justice, community building, and transformation'.[6] Partnership is an essential component of any such attempt to create meaningful social change, and almost a century on from the founding moment of the Gipton social housing estate, new democratic approaches to architectural innovation, in the form of technologies such as MassBespoke, hold the possibility of tackling the local crisis of access to cultural participation.

A conversation between the ELP and BLA began in 2017. At the heart of this partnership are the possibilities presented by the Built InCommon process of distributed fabrication in small community-owned maker spaces. In response to the absence of formal arts spaces and even of any dedicated spaces for creative production (artists'

studios, maker spaces, hack spaces and so on), the idea of creating a maker space, named the 'East Leeds Pavilion', came to the fore. This is imagined as a locally owned and operated space of collective and creative agency, to be designed and constructed using MassBespoke and located at Fearnville Fields on the edge of the Wyke Beck Valley in Gipton. The process is steered by a project team comprising the ELP, BLA, local residents, artists and makers. The prospect of local people taking ownership over the design, construction and operation of the Pavilion has potential to generate social value and stimulate alternative economies in an area where new contemporary approaches to neighbourhood planning and local ownership are yet to make tangible inroads.

Previously, conversations about contemporary art did not resonate across east Leeds. However, a broadening of the definition of 'making', to incorporate everything from growing and baking to more traditional arts and crafts, was adopted. This democratising move ensured accessibility to the project

and helped it to achieve its aims to reach a wider demographic.

Research into existing community infrastructure was an essential starting point in promoting the Pavilion initiative. In effect this is the Plan stage of formulating a social value strategy, mapping assets that we already have. Suspecting that individual makers were likely to be dispersed across east Leeds, but 'hidden' due to the absence of creative venues and networks, over the last year the ELP and BLA have worked together to map this creative landscape, identifying need and potential partners.

Such mapping techniques have already been trialled by BLA in one of their case studies of a Built InCommon research project in the Bagneux neighbourhood of Paris. Working with local civic organisation R-Urban, all the actors within the community that are already working to generate social value and could be potential partners in the Built InCommon project were mapped. The mapping also then allowed the core stakeholders for the project to be identified. A similar process was undertaken for the proposed East Leeds

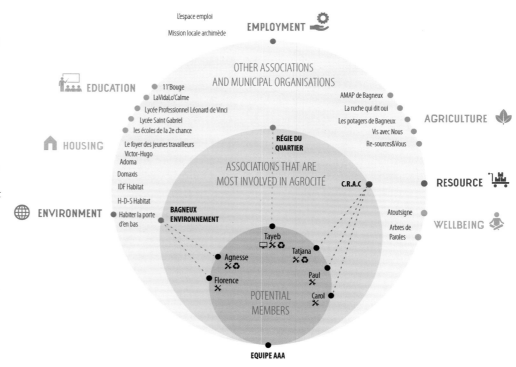

R-Urban and Bauman Lyons Architects, Built InCommon flying factory project, Bagneux, Paris, France, 2018

above: A diagram of information extracted from the mapping of the Built InCommon ecology in Bagneux, illustrating different modes of engagement of the range of identified stakeholders.

opposite: Potential actors and local dynamics, a representation method of the existing ecology of like-minded civic groups and public institutions within the neighbourhood that could support and be enhanced by the provision of a flying factory.

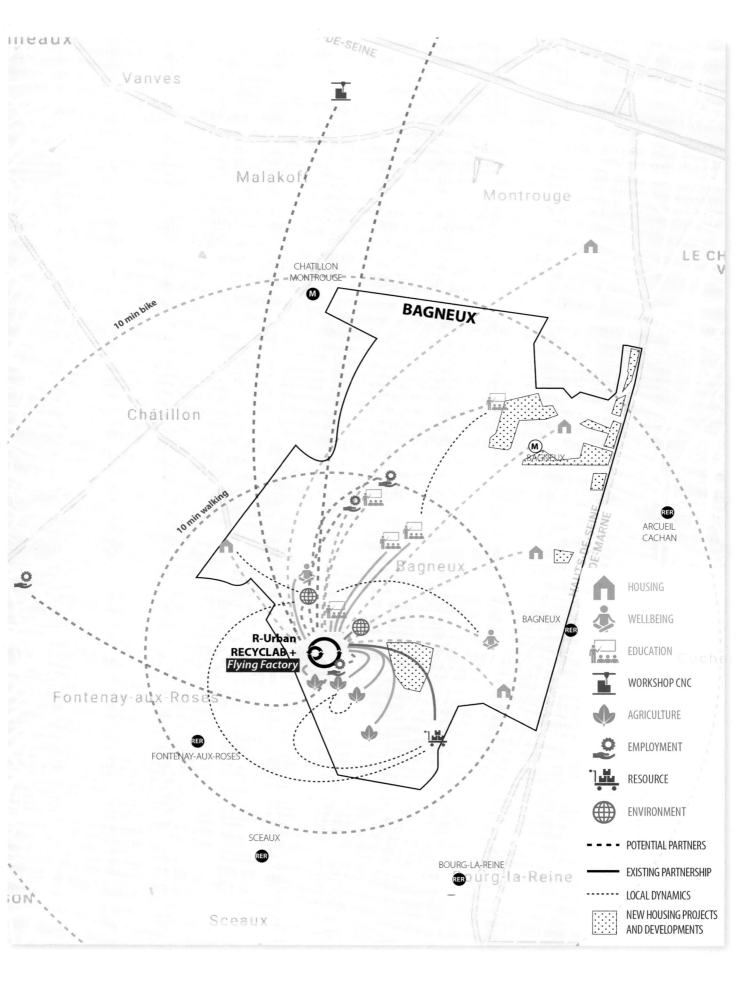

BAGNEUX

CHATILLON
MONTROUGE

10 min bike

10 min walking

R-Urban
RECYCLAB +
Flying Factory

BAGNEUX

ARCUEIL
CACHAN

BAGNEUX

FONTENAY-AUX-ROSES

SCEAUX

SCEAUX

BOURG-LA-REINE

Vanves

Malakoff

Montrouge

Châtillon

Fontenay-aux-Roses

Bagneux

HOUSING

WELLBEING

EDUCATION

WORKSHOP CNC

AGRICULTURE

EMPLOYMENT

RESOURCE

ENVIRONMENT

- - - - POTENTIAL PARTNERS

———— EXISTING PARTNERSHIP

········ LOCAL DYNAMICS

NEW HOUSING PROJECTS
AND DEVELOPMENTS

43

Pavilion, extending the mapping to include individual makers.

The qualitative research, carried out across a year-long period from 2018 to 2019, utilised a mixed methodology based on an online survey; one-to-one interviews with makers and individuals working within local arts and third-sector initiatives; and the project *What Makes Gipton?* devised by the artist Andy Abbott. This employed various platforms for engagement including social events for local makers and a sculptural installation which was launched at the Gipton Gala in July 2019, utilising augmented reality to share digital content related to the makers' work. Interviews used a snowballing technique employed effectively within a parallel research initiative focusing on the inner-east area of the 'rim' neighbourhoods around the centre of Leeds in 2010–11 which highlighted the high concentration of community facilities and social capital in some of the most deprived wards. The technique was adapted for the Gipton project and started with mapping known community institutions and individual projects in the neighbourhood. Interviews began with known individuals working within partner organisations across east Leeds, including arts and third-sector organisations Chapel FM, Gipsil and Space2, whose long-term presence in the area already generates significant social value. The aim of the snowballing technique is to 'talk to further rounds of people, moving further away from well-known people in each round'.[7]

Nine in-depth interviews were conducted during July 2019, which focused on discussion of local landmarks, in particular community infrastructure and assets, as well as potential areas for further development. This first round of interviews solicited new discoveries: while many physical spaces emerging from the research were already known, the process shed light on a multitude of community networks, groups and associations that were not as readily visible prior to the mapping process, and these provide strong links for future involvement with the Pavilion. As one example, snowballing facilitated connection to the 'Manbassadors' project, a growing network of local businesses acting as men's health advocates in east Leeds, reaching out to those who are isolated and aiming to tackle the high levels of suicide among men in the Leeds LS9 postcode area.[8] The Pavilion may in future generate social value through an offer of another means of supporting local men who are isolated but potentially hold valuable skills learned in former careers in the construction industry.

The welcome introduction of a focus on social value, through the partnership with BLA, presents an important intervention for the work of the ELP. Micro creative organisations can find themselves trapped within narrow debates on cultural value based on an arts funder-oriented set of metrics that prioritise measures such as economic impact and footfall. These play to the strengths of larger arts organisations inhabiting major city-centre venues, rather than the alternative practices of those working at the geographic and conceptual margins. But as the AHRC Cultural Value Project noted in 2016, larger and more formal cultural spaces are not always the most effective generators of social value: 'Far more significant might be the effect of small-scale cultural assets – studios, live-music venues, small galleries and so on – in supporting healthier and more balanced communities.'[9]

opposite:
Bauman Lyons Architects, Rim Study, Leeds, England, 2010

Mapping was used in layers to analyse the assets available within the ring of the most deprived neighbourhoods in Leeds. This layer shows the concentration of community facilities. A correlation was found between the density of facilities and the strength of social capital within different communities.

Andy Abbott,
What Makes Gipton?,
Gipton Gala,
East Leeds,
14 July 2019

above: Artist Andy Abbott demonstrates the use of augmented reality to animate a sculptural installation presented at the Gala. Commissioned by the East Leeds Project, it sought to showcase the work of local makers and to engage visitors in dialogue about the proposed East Leeds Pavilion.

right: The research team utilised the presence of Andy Abbott's sculptural installation at the Gala as a springboard to wider conversations with local people about access to community assets across east Leeds. Knowledge was effectively co-produced through these conversations and mapped 'live' onto physical maps during the event.

Mapping the Social Value of Built InCommon: The Next Step

It is critical to the concept of Built InCommon as exemplified by Bagneux and the East Leeds Pavilion that new means continue to be sought for embedding social impact thinking in the creation of services, products and developments. This can be achieved by gathering, assessing and sharing the creation of social value as an alternative to growth-oriented narratives elsewhere within the cultural field and developing mapping techniques to visualise and valorise the social value generated in delivering the project and the post-completion impact.
This is the next stage of mapping to support development of the East Leeds Pavilion. ∆

Notes
1. Kate Pickett and Richard Wilkinson, *The Spirit Level*, Allen Lane (London), 2009.
2. Kate Pickett and Richard Wilkinson interviewed by Dawn Foster, *The Guardian*, 18 September 2018: www.theguardian. com/inequality/2018/sep/18/kate-pickett-richard-wilkinson-mental-wellbeing-inequality-the-spirit-level.
3. 'Built InCommon – Explainer': https://vimeo.com/blakehouse/ download/359013255/bfa1898225.
4. Social Value UK, *Maximise Your Impact: A Guide for Social Entrepreneurs*, 2017: www.socialvalueuk.org/app/uploads/2017/10/ MaximiseYourImpact.24.10.17.pdf
5. Leeds City Council Intelligence and Policy Service, 'Leeds Index of Multiple Deprivation (IMD) 2019': https://storymaps.arcgis.com/ stories/f74f5a2392854990a2db7b685e3151ab
6. Gregory Sholette and Chloë Bass, *Art as Social Action: An Introduction to the Principles and Practices of Teaching Social Practice Art*, Allworth Press (New York), 2018, p xiii.
7. Rachael Unsworth, *Margins Within the City: Social Networks, Under-utilised Space and Under-valued Enterprise*, Leeds Love It Share It CIC (Leeds), 2011, p 35.
8. Sue Wylie, 'Feel Good Factors Manbassadors – All in a Day's Work', 28 July 2019: www.fgfleeds.org/feel-good-factor-manbassadors/
9. Geoffrey Crossick and Patrycja Kaszynska, *Understanding the Value of Arts & Culture: The AHRC Cultural Value Project*, Arts and Humanities Research Council (London), 2016, p 8.

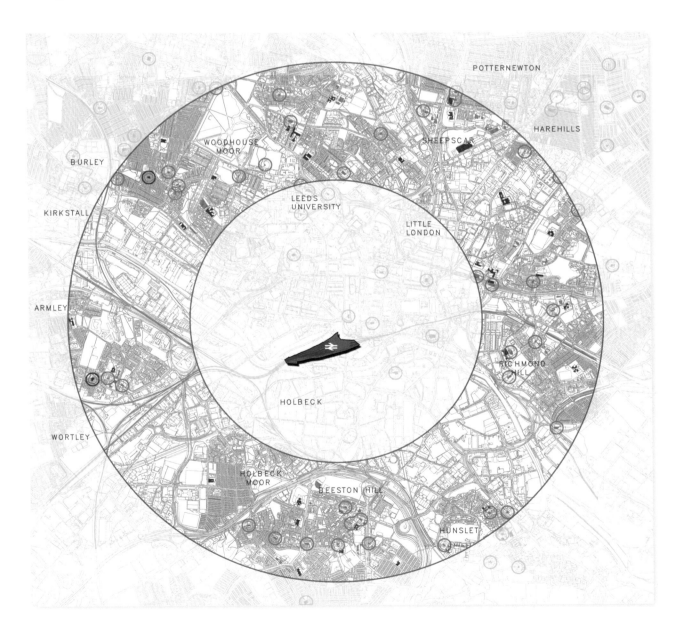

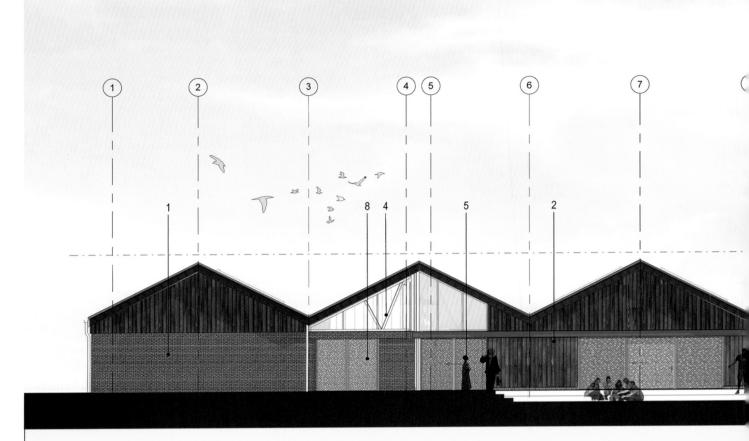

'Engender the Confidence to Demand Better'

The Value of Architects in Community Asset Transfers

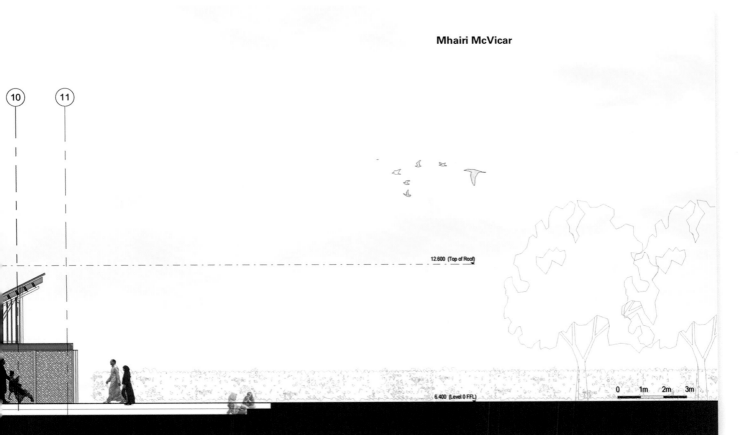

Mhairi McVicar is Reader at the Welsh School of Architecture in Cardiff and Academic Lead of Community Gateway, an organisation that seeks to link Cardiff academics and design professionals with residents and businesses in the city's Grangetown district through a spirit of strong, proactive support. One initiative has been the rejuvenation of the dilapidated Grange Bowls Pavilion and its asset transfer to the local community.

IBI Group and Dan Benham Architect,
Grange Pavilion,
Grangetown, Cardiff, Wales,
2019

A 2017 planning-stage proposal for the redevelopment of the Grange Pavilion project, identifying the brick and timber material palette.

In 2012, a group of residents in Grangetown, Cardiff, Wales, began meeting around kitchen tables to discuss what they could do about several deteriorating buildings around a popular neighbourhood park, including the 1960s Grange Bowls Pavilion, vacated following local authority cutbacks. 'The situation,' the local authority noted of austerity, 'demands a creative response.'[1] The Royal Institute of British Architects (RIBA) similarly identified a need for creative responses to England's Localism Act 2011, writing that the formalisation of community consultation should serve as 'a signal to architects that their skills are valuable'.[2] 'Localism needs design professionals to succeed,' RIBA's *Guide to Localism* advised, 'but the quality of the places created by this new process will be dependent on their ability to appropriately engage with local people and local issues, right from the beginning, designing "with" rather than "for" communities.'[3]

Community asset transfer processes, whereby civic assets are devolved from central or local authorities to community organisations, pose challenges for client and architect alike. RIBA's coupling of quality to long-term engagement is tested by the difficulty fledgling community organisations face in accessing early-stage funding. 'You may,' a local authority advises community groups, 'be able to secure some "pro-bono" work (provided by professionals at no charge).'[4] In this context, how is the value of the architect, and of architecture created through long-term engagement, to be measured?

'We want,' residents leading the Grange Pavilion project affirmed, 'a relationship, and not an affair.'[5] A relationship between residents, organisations, architectural educators, architectural students, and a professional design team

Co-producing a community asset: Grange Pavilion,
Cardiff, Wales,
2013

Since 2013, workshops, ideas picnics, daily drop-ins and annual events between members of the numerous communities within Grangetown, the Welsh School of Architecture, and Cardiff University's Community Gateway have informed and defined the design brief and business case for the Grange Pavilion.

comprising Dan Benham Architect, IBI Group and BECT construction emerged through the seven-year evolution of the Grange Pavilion project.[6] Supported by Cardiff University's Community Gateway[7] and a RIBA Research Trust Award,[8] collective research and teaching is mapping the value of the architect in supporting the activation and long-term management of a social space. Taking up the expansion of architectural praxis outlined in Nishat Awan, Tatjana Schneider and Jeremy Till's 2011 book *Spatial Agency*,[9] architectural skills and ways of thinking are deployed to work with the project long before, during and after the architectural design of a building.

'It's not about the visions but about how they understand the "us" of us,'[10] a resident voiced of the group's expectations of architects. To begin understanding the 'us' of us, three years of architectural teaching and research supported the growth of a partnership through ideas picnics, walks, storytelling events, and open and invited workshops. Residents, academics and students paired up to train as appreciative inquiry researchers, employing asset-based approaches to identify existing physical and social assets rather than seeking problems to be fixed. 'Think carefully about how you portray our community,'[11] residents advised, as qualitative and quantitative analyses of interest, needs and resources offered evidence for funding of one-off events, a two-year residency and, eventually, a 99-year lease under a community asset transfer.

Early architectural interventions through the construction of a storytelling booth and a first-phase renovation offered crucial space and time for individuals and organisations to activate what urban ethnographer Suzanne Hall refers to as the 'conviviality and conflict' of a civic space.[12] The residency gathered a community for the site and physically tested a multitude of uses to incrementally inform an architectural brief and business case for redevelopment. '(Social) space is a (social) product,'[13] Henri Lefebvre declared in *The Production of Space*, writing of the 'coming-into-being' of spatial codes through the establishment of a common language, a consensus and a code. At the Grange Pavilion, a common code was defined through the social activation of a vacant space, supported, step by step, by architectural interventions.

In 2016, the Grange Pavilion Project, constituted as a partnership between residents and community, third-sector and public organisations, selected an architectural team. Expectations that architects should 'raise the quality of the question' sat alongside fears that architects would impose a 'big glass shiny box' and abandon the group to the long-term consequences. 'Who would we trust to come and sort out the mess afterwards, when it is a year down the line and it is not working?' the group questioned. 'Who is going to correct the correction that needs to be made?' The architects' value was conceived in terms of anticipating the long-term social consequences of the quality of a public space. 'Please describe,' the group's Quality Criterion for selection questioned, 'how your team's definitions of architectural quality will respond to the communities' needs.'

In a neighbourhood routinely defined by multiple deprivation index rankings, quality was central to residents' ambitions for the long-term social, physical and economic

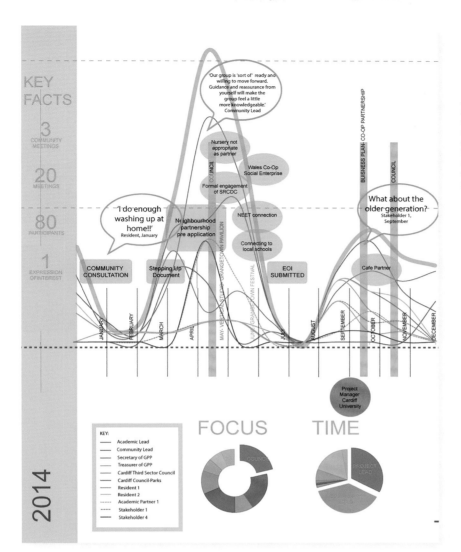

Sarah Ackland,
Measuring one year of
a community asset transfer,
Welsh School of Architecture,
Cardiff, Wales,
2016

A 2015 RIBA Research Trust award supported a detailed mapping of the demands that a community asset transfer process places on time, skills and resources. An analysis of one year of email communications between key partners over 2014 identified the ebb and flow of momentum, barriers hit, and the catalytic effect of regular public events to grow a project partnership.

Welsh asset mapping,
BSc3 Grangetown Unit,
Welsh School of Architecture,
Cardiff, Wales,
2017

Architectural teaching and research in the Welsh School of Architecture has adopted an asset-based approach informed by 'appreciative inquiry' principles, locating existing physical, social and cultural assets rather than seeking 'problems' to be 'fixed'.

IBI Group and
Dan Benham Architect,
Grange Pavilion,
Grangetown,
Cardiff, Wales,
2019

The Grange Pavilion is located in a
neighbourhood park in Grangetown and
includes three multi-purpose spaces of
varying sizes to support a social enterprise
cafe run by a local business, and an
outdoor classroom. Landscaping by the
Cardiff-based urban design company
the Urbanists provides surface-drainage
rain gardens throughout the site,
and anticipates ongoing resident-led
development of the landscape.

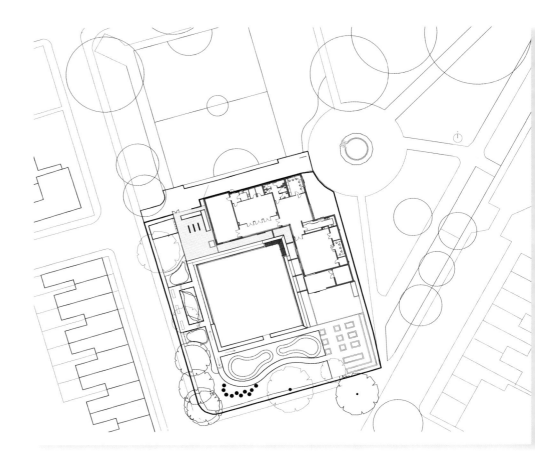

Welsh School of Architecture x St Patrick's Primary + Cathays High

IBI Group and Dan Benham Architect,
Grange Pavilion,
Grangetown, Cardiff, Wales,
2019

top: The extended design team included BECT construction, who worked closely with the Grange Pavilion CIO, residents, the design team and students, supporting the presence of a resident artist and an architectural student research intern whose work mapped concepts of care throughout construction, as well as a series of site visits, including this one for architecture students as they began working with artist Chris Williams to prototype furnishings from resident-defined briefs.

above: The outdoor classroom and landscape will be used by adjacent landlocked primary schools, with site biodiversity encouraged by bee, bird and bat bricks built into the facade, and swallow- and bat-friendly eaves. Biodiversity activities on site will be supported by Grange Pavilion CIO member organisation RSPB Cymru.

Isabella Open and Matthew Gaunt,
My Grange Pavilion,
MArch2 Value Unit,
Welsh School of Architecture,
Cardiff, Wales,
2018–19

opposite: Welsh School of Architecture BSc and MArch students partnered annually with residents and organisations of the Grange Pavilion Charitable Incorporated Organisation (CIO) to support each stage of design, construction and activation. In 2018–19, MArch2 students and BSc1 and 2 students developed detailed written specifications and drawings of each space as described in interviews with the groups and individuals who will inhabit them.

value of a public space which will serve 20,000 residents over a 99-year lease. Definitions of quality beyond cost-per-square-metre metrics is supported by economic theories and UK Government policies which advocate, at least on paper, fundamental shifts in value measurement. The Public Services (Social Value) Act 2012 requires public-sector organisations to look beyond financial cost to consider wider economic, social and environmental wellbeing.[14] The Well-being of Future Generations (Wales) Act 2015 requires public bodies to demonstrate 'the importance of balancing short-term needs with the need to safeguard the ability to also meet long-term needs.'[15] Mariana Mazzucato's *The Value of Everything* (2018) proposes that we 'reconsider the stories we are telling about who the value creators are, and what that says to us about how we define activities as economically productive and unproductive.'[16]

As the Grange Pavilion progresses from concept to construction and inhabitation, the partnership between residents, organisations, architects, educators and students continues to pursue the measurement of the social value of a public space. Emerging from a context in which *Spon's First Stage Estimating Handbook* published 'community centres' as costing between 62 and 55 per cent of the value of luxury flats,[17] in which RIBA explicitly aligns architectural quality to early engagement but in which lack of resourcing anticipates pro-bono services, and in which community groups expect that architects should 'engender the confidence to demand better',[18] a reconsideration of the stories we tell about the social value of architecture is timely. ∆

Notes
1. Cardiff Council, *STEPPING UP: A Toolkit for Developing and Managing Services and Asset*, 2014, p 4: www.cardiff.gov.uk/ENG/resident/Schools-and-learning/Services-for-young-people/Commissioning-Youth-Service/Documents/Stepping%20Up%20Toolkit.pdf.
2. Angela Brady, 'Foreword', *RIBA Guide to Localism Part 2: Getting Community Engagement Right*, RIBA (London), p 1.
3. 'Introduction', *RIBA Guide to Localism Part 2: Getting Community Engagement Right*, RIBA (London), p 2.
4. STEPPING UP, *op cit*, p 12.
5. Resident, 2012.
6. The Pavilion and landscape were funded by National Lottery, Welsh Government, Enabling Natural Resources Wales, Moondance Foundation, Garfield Weston, HEFCW, Cardiff Bay Rotary and area business and individual donations.
7. www.cardiff.ac.uk/community-gateway.
8. RIBA Research Trust Award 2015: 'The Value of the Architect in a Community Asset Transfer', Mhairi McVicar and Neil Turnbull.
9. Nishat Awan, Tatjana Schneider, Jeremy Till, *Spatial Agency: Other Ways of Doing Architecture*, Routledge (London and New York), 2011, pp 28–9.
10. Resident, 2016.
11. Resident, 2013.
12. Suzanne Hall, *City, Street and Citizen: The Measure of the Ordinary*, Routledge (London and New York), 2012, p 5.
13. Henri Lefebvre, *The Production of Space*, trans Donald Nicholson-Smith, Blackwell (Oxford; Cambridge, MA), 1991, p 26.
14. Public Services (Social Value) Act 2011.
15. Welsh Government, *Well-being of Future Generations (Wales) Act 2015: The Essentials*, p 7: https://futuregenerations.wales/about-us/future-generations-act/.
16. Mariana Mazzucato, *The Value of Everything: Making and Taking in the Global Economy*, Allen Lane (London), 2018, p 19.
17. Bryan JD Spain, *Spon's First Stage Estimating Handbook*, Spon Press (London), third edition, 2010, p 3.
18. Resident, 2016.

CONNECTION - SOCIAL AND DIGITAL

MAPPING
ECO-

POSITIVE EMOTIONS - ASPIRATION AND IDENTITY

MINDFULNESS - NATURE AND WELLBEING

MESA,
Eco-social map highlighting key assets
and suggestions for improvement,
Orts Road Estate and Newtown,
Reading, England, 2019

When the individual layers are compared, it can be observed that connection is fairly localised to the neighbourhood, whereas active lifestyles depend upon facilities across the town. Positive emotions and mindfulness are closely aligned with green and blue spaces, and the changes suggested through flexibility and freedom relate not only to local places, but also to connections to the science park to the east.

ACTIVE LIFESTYLES - RECREATION AND LEISURE

SOCIAL ASSETS

FLEXIBILTY AND FREEDOM - CHANGES AND IMPROVEMENTS

Cartography is a very powerful tool. Maps can reveal hidden potential, redefine the hierarchy of knowledge, and provoke social change. Guest-Editor **Eli Hatleskog** describes how at Reading University, the Department of Architecture's Mapping Eco Social Assets (MESA) strategies have provoked ideas for improvements to the city, but have also stressed the importance of focal buildings such as schools and places of worship that generate community cohesion.

Maps are not benign representations of the world; they can construct knowledge and even promote social change. Some qualities are easier to map than others; things that can be measured and counted are often privileged over intangible assets. In order to develop a more joined-up understanding of the built environment it seems clear that social value must have a role to play. Through mapmaking, the Newton-funded Mapping Eco Social Assets (MESA) project at the School of Architecture, University of Reading, has provided a framework for a collaborative inquiry into social value in context.

MESA began in 2018 with the aim of exploring some of the complex challenges around understanding and developing social assets in the built environment, teasing out the nuances underpinning a parallel industry-facing strand of MESA's work – the Social Value Toolkit for Architecture. A methodology for promoting, capturing and monetising the social impact of design,[1] the pilot study was initiated at Orts Road and Newtown in Reading, Berkshire, to develop practical methods for evidencing social value at the neighbourhood scale. Rather than placing emphasis solely on monetary proxies, MESA studied varying perceptions and definitions of social value and how these interact spatially across different publics and places. Across communities, one-size-fits-all approaches are not appropriate. Instead, there is a need for localised conversations, interpretations and variations.

The Social Value of Local Networks
Local knowledge was key to the project, so the first aim was to find collaborators. After numerous attempts to make connections, ranging from contacting churches, charities and schools to staging street surveys, it was clear that those who had been approached had neither the time nor the inclination to get involved. The project seemed to be at an impasse. However, a phone call changed everything. Reading Borough Council's Neighbourhood Initiatives Officer had received an email regarding the project and wanted to hear more. The moment was serendipitous, since the council had recently completed a survey of its tenants at the Orts Road Estate to learn if cutbacks had affected the ways in which they perceived the area, and also to address concerns about wellbeing. If MESA could help to support conversations with residents about social value in the neighbourhood, then there were clear advantages to working together. Taking a holistic view, increased social value in the built environment could lead to reductions in antisocial behaviour, which costs the council in many different ways, ranging from the time of council officers,

Mapping Eco Social Assets (MESA) project site,
Orts Road and Newtown,
Reading, England,
2019

The University of Reading's MESA project, based at the School of Architecture,
studied a site in the town bounded by railway tracks to the northeast and the
Kennet and Avon Canal to the northwest. The red line highlights a political
ward boundary that runs down the middle of the neighbourhood.

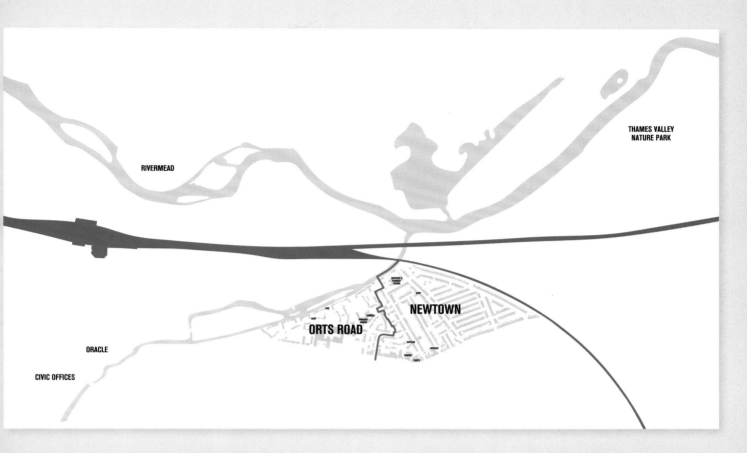

RIVERMEAD

THAMES VALLEY
NATURE PARK

NEWTOWN

ORTS ROAD

ORACLE

CIVIC OFFICES

police and social services, to the broader impact for communities.

Across Europe, universities are under increasing scrutiny to justify their value and give back to society. In response to this, the 'Civic University' model, as described by John Goddard, aims 'to capture the mutually beneficial engagement between the community, region or wider world and the university'.[2] The approach suggests that novel ways of combining research, teaching and engagement must be developed and that these can lead to more responsive, evidence-based approaches to growth and development. In Reading, the Borough Council shared deep local knowledge, networks and practical experience of working in the town, and MESA provided resources, expertise and research methods. A site-specific response to research and engagement has thus been developed that may set the scene for future collaborations.

Context

Reading was shaped in no small way by biscuits. At its peak in the 1900s, the town's Huntley & Palmers biscuit factory was the largest in the world. Mass-produced biscuits were distributed along the Kennet and Avon Canal. Across the canal, workers' housing was built at Newtown.[3] The western side of Newtown was of

poor stock and was replaced by the Orts Road Estate in the late 1980s. The red-brick estate has some playful postmodern flourishes, set amongst a warren of arches, pathways and blind corners. The remaining part of the original Newtown is typified by its terraced houses, a reminder of how the whole area used to look when the air smelt of biscuits.

Orts Road and Newtown share key amenities, such as two primary schools, shops and religious buildings, and enjoy close access to parks and waterways. They are, however, divided in economy and demographics. Orts Road has a mix of providers of social housing, ranging from the local authority to housing associations. In Newtown, housing is privately owned or rented. Newtown is home to a broader demographic, with younger families in their first homes and older owner-occupiers. To compound the divide, a political ward boundary runs down the middle of the site, separating the estate (Labour) from Newtown (Green Party). The result of this is that six councillors represent the small neighbourhood.

Locating Social Assets

Part of the challenge of engaging with residents at Orts Road and Newtown was that there were no established community groups or organisations. This is where

Reading Borough Council stepped in, by allowing MESA to tag a mapping workshop onto a council-run event. The event took place in the lounge of a sheltered-housing facility. Once the council had disseminated the results of its tenant survey and discussed responses such as recycling and maintenance, activities moved on to a large-format map of the neighbourhood.

A series of workshops were structured around prompts relating to the Social Value Toolkit and its initial themes of connection, active lifestyles, positive emotions, taking notice/mindfulness, and flexibility and freedom, and developed to encourage group discussions through the shared activity of locating assets on a map. Participants were asked, for example, to think about where they tended to stop and talk to people, where their local shops and services were, where they felt happiest, and also what they found beautiful in their surroundings. They were also encouraged to write notes onto the map and discuss their responses as a group. Towards the end of the mapping part of the workshops, group analysis of the map included collective reflections on why certain areas were of interest. The activities then led to broader discussions about practical measures that could be taken to improve social value locally over the next few years, and concluded with the writing of imagined headlines about what participants would like the area to be famous for in 10 years' time.

The structure of the workshops led to rich and varied discussions about the built environment. The positive nature of the questions turned conversations away from complaints about antisocial behaviour towards reflections on the places where a heron could be seen or the beauty of the canal. Neighbourhood consultations tend not to be focused on current assets and aimed towards building arguments for or against a specific change or development. The nature of MESA's engagement was therefore unusual, since there was no proposal, just a few questions. In total, around 200 people took part in mapmaking workshops, ranging from primary-school children to young adults, parents and pensioners.

In addition to the mapping workshops, MESA collaborated with Reading Borough Council in the planning of another outdoor community event on a small green on the Orts Road Estate. Ward councillors ran an outdoor surgery and consultations on a new proposed play area, with free ice cream, a bouncy castle and stalls. MESA used the event not only to run more mapmaking activities, but also to gather feedback on the earlier maps and project. An emerging theme raised by

MESA mapping workshop,
Weirside Court,
Orts Road Estate,
Reading, England,
2018

The workshop took place at a sheltered-housing facility where participants were asked to locate social assets on a map and mark them with stickers, which revealed that local places such as the pub and cafe were appreciated, along with the biodiversity along the canal.

MESA mapping workshop,
Weirside Court,
Orts Road Estate,
Reading, England,
2019

During a workshop with a group of Scouts at St Johns and St Stephen's Church, measures to make the area better were discussed, from filling in potholes to building a swimming pool, and providing spaces where they could be trusted to be without adult supervision.

all age groups was a lack of local sports and recreation activities, so an outdoor table-tennis table was acquired from a charity and placed next to the MESA stall. It was subsequently donated to the community and is now housed in a local community centre – one simple and unexpected way in which research funds can be used to generate social impact.

Holistic Mapping for Decision-Making

The workshop maps were redrawn for ease of comparison. The process followed a simple yet consistent set of rules and the result was a multilayer vector drawing, a composite map highlighting where intangible and tangible assets interacted and overlapped spatially. It was, however, a busy and confusing jumble of assets that lacked any real usefulness without further analysis. It was at this point in the project that there was a shift from community mapping towards considerations of urban systems and joined-up approaches to planning and development.

The edges of a site are more than just a line on a map. One of the challenges of the Reading project has been the delineation of social site boundaries, which was done through a process of negotiation. Following group analysis, feedback from stakeholders, the local authority

and networks such as Reading 2050, it became clear that the eco-social values at Orts Road and Newtown were not only linked to other parts of the town, but also to adjoining Wokingham Borough Council.

The MESA maps were structured in colour-coded layers representing not only different demographics, but also Social Value Toolkit themes, with each layer given a transparency. This supported visual analysis, since where assets were most often mentioned the hue was darkest, and where themes and assets overlapped, new colours were created. In turn, layers could be switched off and on to see how different types of values were distributed. Blue revealed the desire for more connectivity, both digital and social, in the spaces between buildings. Orange showed that recreation and leisure opportunities were typically too far away. Red and yellow combined in places since mindfulness and positive emotions were closely aligned, focusing on parks, recreational spaces and waterways, as well as religious and educational buildings. In turn, green demonstrated that the improvements that resonated most locally related to safety, autonomy, skills and aspiration.

In order to understand social value in a complex and rich environment, MESA took its starting point quite simply in asking people what they valued most about

MESA used the event not only to run more mapmaking activities, but also to gather feed- back on the earlier maps and project

MESA community mapping event, Orts Road Estate, Reading, England, 2019
.

As part of a neighbourhood fun day organised by Reading Borough Council, MESA staged an outdoor mapping event with recreational activities for adults and children. On one of the hottest days of the summer, there were around 100 visitors, many of whom took part in mapmaking and consultations.

The maps spatially represent workshop data in a visual and accessible way. They have supported debate and discussions about social value among different council departments and also across political and ward divides

MESA,
Eco-social overview map,
Orts Road Estate and Newtown,
Reading, England,
2019

Each mapping workshop was given its own layer in the eco-social map. These semi-transparent social layers were overlaid with layers representing the built and natural environment to create a composite image for subsequent analysis.

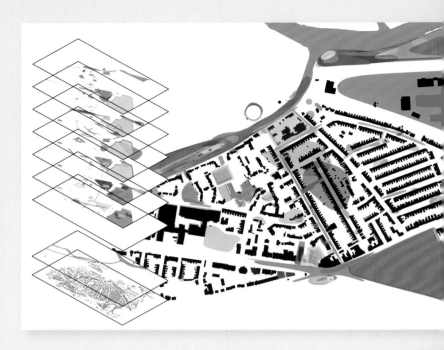

MESA,
Neighbourhood links to the town and surroundings,
Orts Road Estate and Newtown, Reading, England,
2019

Following analysis of the workshop maps, it became clear that social value was not simply contained on site, but dependent on connections to and relationships with the broader area.

KEY

CONNECTION - SOCIAL AND DIGITAL
ACTIVE LIFESTYLES - RECREATION AND LEISURE
POSITIVE EMOTIONS - ASPIRATION AND IDENTITY
MINDFULNESS - NATURE AND WELLBEING
FLEXIBILTY AND FREEDOM - CHANGES AND IMPROVEMENTS
PROPOSED NEW HOUSING
WATERWAYS
RAILWAY LINES

MESA,
Eco-social map highlighting key
assets and suggestions for improvement,
Orts Road Estate and Newtown, Reading, England,
2019

The resultant eco-social map reveals how the opinions of around 200 people overlap across the area. The map highlights the value of school and religious buildings, and reveals places that might be improved on (in green).

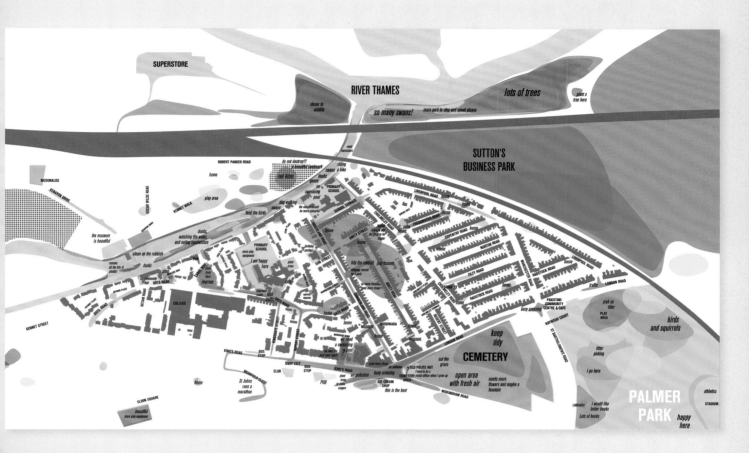

their local area. Conversations were structured around the planning and making of eco-social value maps of the area, developed as a way of evidencing social value in the built environment, with an emphasis on positive, existing assets. With regards to the future, from the point of view of the Neighbourhood Initiatives Officer who helped to facilitate the process, when asked she stated that ideally she 'would like the project to genuinely affect planning decisions. There are more and more pressures on development, but people need more than just homes, they also need places to live with happy and rewarding connections to their community.'[4]

The maps spatially represent workshop data in a visual and accessible way. They have supported debate and discussions about social value among different council departments and also across political and ward divides. This has led to the development of local planning guidance that pinpoints appropriate sites for improvements and interventions with the maximum potential to enhance social value locally.

The planning system in the UK has long been criticised for being too reactive. In turn, public consultations often happen too late in the development process for meaningful engagement. MESA has demonstrated that collaboratively locating social assets and value amongst communities can not only

help local authorities make informed choices based on social and environmental as well as economic value, but also provide new opportunities for them to better understand the communities they serve. The MESA team has since been presented with a range of opportunities for further projects and funding. The project is therefore also a call to architects to become more entrepreneurial and proactive in their approach to getting new work through the development of relevant social research with communities. ∞

Notes
1. 'RIBA Social Value Toolkit': https://www.architecture.com/knowledge-and-resources/resources-landing-page/social-value-toolkit.
2. John Goddard, 'What Do We Mean By the "Civic University"? Why is it Important?', European Economic and Social Committee, 13 June 2014: www.eesc.europa.eu/resources/docs/what-do-we-mean-by-the-civic-university.pdf.
3. 'Revealing Reading's Hidden History: Orts Road and Newtown': http://happymuseumproject.org/wp-content/uploads/2013/07/RRH-Orts-leaflet-for-website-2.pdf.
4. Ebony George, Neighbourhood Initiatives Officer, Reading Borough Council, interview with the author, Reading council offices, 11 November 2019.

Changing Patterns of Resilience

Exploring the Local

The notion of resilience is often referred to in relation to data services or the effects of climate change. However, understanding of social resilience and how it can vary across urban districts over time is vital too. Social Life co-founder **Nicola Bacon** and data scientist **Paul Goodship** outline the research organisation's resilience mapping with the London Borough of Hounslow, which supported a better understanding of community dynamics and decision-making.

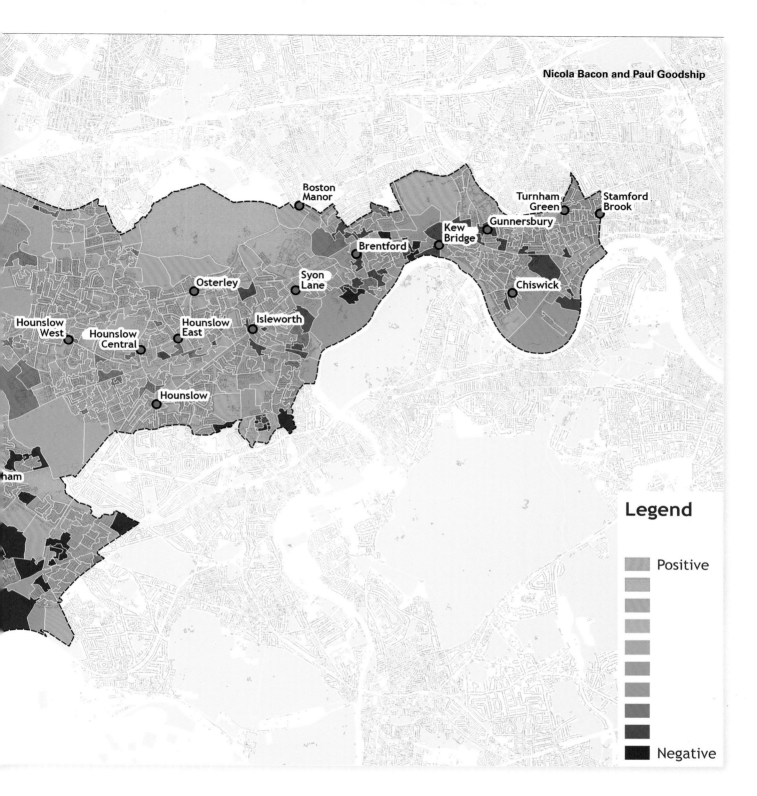

Legend

Positive

Negative

Social Life,
Predicted resilience across the
London Borough of Hounslow,
2015

Darker blue represents lower predicted resilience,
and darker orange higher predicted resilience. This
shows how areas with lower predicted resilience are
more common in the west of the borough, with areas
of high predicted resilience concentrated in the east.
The centre of the borough is more likely to be neither
high nor low in predicted resilience.

Understanding resilience is critical to our analysis of how communities manage and respond to changes at a local level, and how public authorities can best intervene and support local neighbourhoods. This is particularly relevant in those places, like many in the UK, where both scarce and reducing public-sector spending, and population growth and churn, risk fragmenting communities and undermining their ability to cope.

Social Life, an independent research organisation set up by the Young Foundation in 2012, specialises in research and community projects exploring how we are affected by changes in the built environment, focusing on the relationship between people and place. In 2015 the organisation was approached by the London Borough of Hounslow to develop a fresh way of modelling community resilience using existing data. The work was extended in 2018 to explore change over time and the impact of migration and population churn on Hounslow's local neighbourhoods. The report, *A New Resilience Model for Hounslow*, was published in 2019.[1]

The Hounslow model is based on an analysis of national survey data, mapped to small areas, and publicly available data describing places, including socioeconomic and deprivation statistics. The tool is designed to support better insight into local areas and their community dynamics, and to support conversations, negotiations and decision-making around resilience. The impact on resilience of built environment interventions is a key element in assessing their social value.

Why Map Resilience?

Social Life's work with the London Borough of Hounslow explored how resilience in the borough's neighbourhoods can be quantified.[2] The aims were to make best use of openly available data describing local areas and how people feel about them to better understand the different factors that support (or undermine) resilience and wellbeing; and to investigate how data reporting residents' perceptions, or predicted perceptions, might sit alongside the maps of deficits or needs more familiar to those involved in shaping the built environment.

The UK is well served by extensive data about population and social needs, and much of this is openly available, including from the Office for National Statistics (ONS), Department for Work and Pensions (DWP), Public Health England and the Department of Education. London is regarded as a leader in open data, as it 'shares an unprecedented amount with its citizens to use as they wish',[3] for example through the London Datastore and Transport for London. What gives London an 'information edge over many other cities is the belief that data can not only record social change, but also instigate it'.[4]

Practitioners and policy makers are becoming increasingly familiar with maps and visualisations of data created by organisations such as the Consumer Data Research Centre.[5] These reveal spatial patterns that help understand inequality and disadvantage, showing both significant regional trends and how, within these, small local areas may differ from surrounding areas.

Hounslow town centre,
London,
2018

The central shopping area in Hounslow. This part of the borough has relatively strong predicted resilience.

For Hounslow, the priority was to better understand the ability of communities to cope with change. The council's key assumption was that resilience can make people and communities less reliant on services. Pinpointing which elements of resilience an area struggles with can enable the council and its partners to identify which interventions to put in place.

Social Life's work on resilience flows from the assumption that neighbourhoods that thrive do so because of their local assets and social wealth, and that these factors are important in supporting people from all backgrounds, particularly those who are vulnerable and disadvantaged. In the same way that some individuals find it easier to deal with life's difficulties and bounce back in the face of problems that may stop others in their tracks, some places have over time proved more resilient to shocks and downturns than others. This is reflected by the World Health Organization's definition of resilience as 'the dynamic process of adapting well and responding individually or collectively in the face of challenging circumstances, economic crisis, psychological stress, trauma, tragedy, threats, and other significant sources of stress'.[6]

Substantial work has been done on individual resilience to ascertain why some individuals recover or flourish when facing adversity or risk better than others. Research, particularly in relation to child and adolescent development, has tried to understand the interplay of biological, psychological and social variables that allow successful adaptation in some individuals. Research on community resilience is less developed, but extends these approaches, based on the premise that 'place matters'.[7] Sir Michael Rutter, the first professor of child psychiatry in the UK, has distinguished between moderating factors that help a person or community thrive, and those that assist them in coping at the time of or after adversity.[8] The focus in Social Life's Hounslow model is on exploring the factors that moderate risk prior to adversity, which are referred to as 'assets'.[9]

The model creates a tool to flag the social aspects of small areas that may fall under the radar and are often hidden within official data revealing both strengths and weaknesses in local communities. The starting point was the Young Foundation's Wellbeing and Resilience Model (WARM), the structure of which was simplified and developed and the data updated.[10]

The insights from the resilience model can help direct public-sector spending and intervention to support communities that are lacking the assets that can help them thrive in the face of an uncertain future. Public-sector resources are becoming increasingly stretched, with 27% of Londoners currently living in poverty (after housing costs).[11] Resilience is critical in understanding how communities manage and respond to stress and change at the local level, and how councils can best intervene to support local neighbourhoods.[12] Quantifying resilience over time is an important element in assessing the social value of interventions in the built environment for the residents living in the areas affected.

The Resilience Model
The resilience model brings together hard data about social needs and conditions with perceptions data on how people feel about their everyday lives (referred to as 'predictive data'). In the areas where the hard data and the predictive data move in different directions, particularly local assets and vulnerabilities come into view. Observations of local areas and conversations with residents and agencies can help throw light on the detail of these very local dynamics.

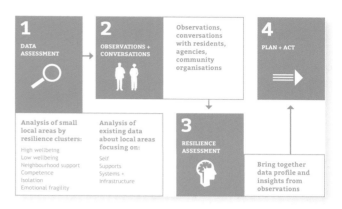

Social Life,
Resilience model process,
2019

Data is assembled and analysed, then corroborated with observations of and interviews with local communities to develop a plan to support both assets and needs in the area.

The predictive data for Hounslow was modelled from the Understanding Society Survey. This is the 'largest longitudinal study of its kind with over 40,000 households included', and 'provides crucial information for researchers and policymakers on the changes and stability of people's lives in the UK'.[13] The data for 2009 and 2015 (the most up-to-date at the time the work was carried out) were analysed. The six-year period spans the introduction and normalisation of public-sector austerity, substantial reductions in supports from councils and other agencies for local residents, changes to welfare benefits and increases in housing costs across London.[14]

Factor analysis, which aims to 'explain high dimensional data with a smaller number of variables',[15] was employed to investigate how different survey questions relate to the core concepts of wellbeing and resilience, and to identify those that constitute wellbeing and resilience measures. A cluster analysis that 'seeks to divide the population into homogeneous subgroups'[16] was then used to group the questions and factors together to develop clusters of respondents with different levels of wellbeing and resilience.

From this analysis, six 'resilience clusters' were identified: 'Low wellbeing' (characterised by lower satisfaction with life overall, income, amount of leisure time, and concerns about managing financially); 'High wellbeing' (higher satisfaction with life overall, income, amount of leisure time, and concerns about managing financially); 'Neighbourhood support' (high social solidarity and high belonging); 'Competence' (high levels of capability and low levels of stress); 'Isolation' (low levels of belonging and local levels of social solidarity); and 'Emotional fragility' (high levels of stress and low levels of capability).

Mapping these clusters to local neighbourhoods in Hounslow highlighted where people with these characteristics are likely to live, and through this identified the predicted resilience of individual neighbourhoods. Using ONS Output Area Classifications (OACs) (each output area typically represents between 110 and 139 households)[17] enabled small areas to be identified where the proportions of people within each cluster are significantly different to the overall proportions. This approach could potentially be extended beyond Hounslow and London to explore trends across wider areas. Clusters can be mapped to OACs across England and Wales to show where particularly high, or low, concentrations of people with the different cluster characteristics are living in a variety of different contexts.

The different datasets available for the two years included the Index of Multiple Deprivation (IMD) 2015,[18] data on fuel poverty and on childhood obesity. Mapping the clusters and datasets demonstrated that, in Hounslow, areas of high predicted resilience were more likely to be less deprived, and low predicted resilience more likely to be deprived. However, the study also revealed areas of high deprivation with low predicted resilience, and areas of low deprivation with high predicted resilience, showing that this relationship is complex.

Several local areas within the borough were visited to explore how the data relates to everyday life, with a particular focus on where the predictive and hard data conflicted. The aim was to explore areas where the data indicated that local assets could be supporting resilience, where the hard data is stronger than the prediction, or where there may be particular vulnerabilities, where predicted strengths are not related in actual data. The visits, conversations with residents and local stakeholders, and observations of physical boundaries,

Social Life,
Neighbourhood support resilience
cluster mapped to Hounslow,
London,
2019

right: How the areas with the highest and lowest predicted neighbourhood support map to Hounslow's neighbourhoods. Areas with higher scores are distributed across the borough, but more common in the east and in the centre.

Social Life,
Emotional fragility resilience
cluster mapped to Hounslow,
London,
2019

below right: How the areas with the highest and lowest predicted emotional fragility resilience map to Hounslow's neighbourhoods. The distribution is broadly similar to the neighbourhood support cluster, where many areas with high predicted neighbourhood support score positively on emotional fragility (meaning that they contain a higher concentration of people with low emotional fragility).

The aim was to explore areas where the data indicated that local assets could be supporting resilience

local assets such as parks and community infrastructure and different housing types or tenures, helped throw light on what emerged from the data analysis.

Around Hanworth Park in the west of the borough, for example, the data revealed adjacent areas of high and low predicted resilience. These were two very different communities side by side: one more affluent, with two- and three-storey homes and a strong local identity separating it from the rest of the borough; the other more isolated, physically divided from neighbouring areas by secure Ministry of Defence housing.

Using the Model Across London

The assessment of the changing resilience of Hounslow between 2009 and 2015 demonstrates that the borough is fragmenting, with the east developing a more resilient community that connects to neighbouring Hammersmith, Ealing and Richmond, and the west and central parts seeing less change. The west remains akin to the southern part of Hillingdon, both neighbouring Heathrow Airport.

Holy Trinity Church,
High Street, Hounslow, London,
2019

The centre of the borough is an area with historically high levels of migration from India and Pakistan.

The visits, conversations with residents and local stakeholders, and observations of physical boundaries, local assets such as parks and community infrastructure and different housing types or tenures, helped throw light on what emerged from the data analysis

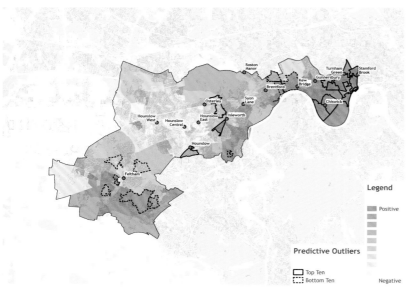

Legend

Positive

Predictive Outliers

Top Ten
Bottom Ten   Negative

Social Life,
IMD and resilience cluster
outliers mapped to Hounslow,
London,
2019

How the areas with the highest and lowest predicted resilience scores (the 'resilience outliers') map against deprivation levels across Hounslow. Dotted lines indicate areas of low predicted resilience, solid lines indicate areas of high predicted resilience.

Local government boundaries do not always either map onto natural neighbourhoods or match the social trends described by the data. The shape of the borough of Hounslow, with its narrow curvature to the east, effectively allows the eastern end to disconnect from the rest and become a larger part of a wider West London area where predicted resilience has strengthened.

This can in part be explained by exploring how these local changes relate to the London-wide picture. A changing pattern in predicted resilience can be observed across the city, especially in inner London, where some areas of weak predicted resilience in 2009 had strengthened by 2015. This is especially noticeable around the fringes, including Chiswick in east Hounslow. Over the same period, a swathe of outer southwest, southeast and east London, plus the fringes of northwest London, are also predicted to have become more resilient.

Demonstrating the Value of the Model

The hardening predicted resilience divide in Hounslow is amplifying longstanding economic and social differences between the less affluent west and centre of the borough and the more prosperous east. Between 2009 and 2015 the east became financially more secure and the west more deprived. However, within this overall pattern there are pockets of inequality. This is starkest around Brentford, where an area of low predicted resilience is boxed in by some of the borough's most resilient and wealthy neighbourhoods.

Brentford is dominated by social housing estates, however a substantial amount of new housing development is bringing people into the area from socioeconomic backgrounds different to many longstanding residents. The impact of this could be to disrupt community networks and supports, and create tensions between new arrivals and more settled

2009

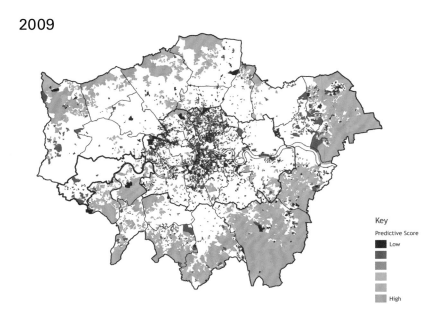

Social Life,
Completed housing
development in Hounslow,
London,
mapped against areas of
low and high predicted
resilience,
2015

opposite: The size of the circle reflects completed numbers of units. Dotted lines indicate areas of low predicted resilience, solid lines indicate areas of high predicted resilience. This illustrates the concentration of new housing development around Brentford, in an area with low predicted resilience, close to Chiswick to the east, which includes many neighbourhoods with high predicted resilience.

Key

Predictive Score

▓ Low

▓ High

Social Life,
Predictive resilience outliers,
London,
2009 and 2015

above and right: How the areas with the highest and lowest predicted resilience score (the 'resilience outliers') comparing 2009 to 2015. Darker blue represents lower predicted resilience, and orange higher predicted resilience.

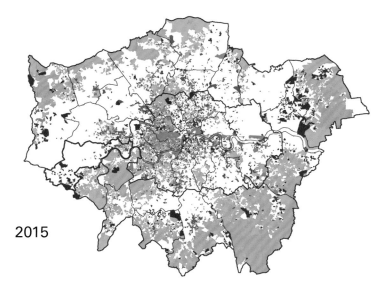

2015

communities – threatening the stability of an already fragile area.

Other regeneration and housing growth areas across London may have low predicted resilience, and like Brentford be facing the pressures of new housing development at scale. This is particularly likely to be the case in areas of higher deprivation where land values are low.

The resilience model reveals the unexpected strengths and weaknesses of an area, highlighting neighbourhoods that may slip under the radar during more standard assessment processes. It can identify areas where the hard data and predictive resilience show different patterns: where a place appears to be thriving despite predicted weaknesses, or where it is likely to be resilient, but in reality appears to be struggling.

The model's strength is in demonstrating what is happening beneath these wider trends to reveal local patterns and sensitivities that may not be visible in more familiar data. This can throw new light on the impact of policy and practice, allowing local authorities and other public-sector agencies to target their scarce resources most effectively. The resilience lens can bring fresh insights into understanding and assessing social value in the built environment. ⌂

Notes
1. Nicola Bacon, Paul Goodship and Alix Naylor, *A New Resilience Model for Hounslow,* Social Life (London), 2019.
2. *Ibid.*
3. James Cheshire and Oliver Uberti, *London: The Information Capital: 100 Maps and Graphics That Will Change How You View the City,* Particular Books (Penguin) (London), 2014, p 21.
4. *Ibid.*
5. www.cdrc.ac.uk/.
6. Jane South *et al, What Qualitative and Quantitative Measures Have Been Developed to Measure Health-related Community Resilience at a National and Local Level? WHO Health Evidence Network Synthesis Report 60,* World Health Organization (Geneva), 2018, p 2.
7. Ruth Lupton, *'Neighbourhood Effects': Can We Measure Them and Does it Matter?* CASE paper 73, Centre for Analysis of Social Exclusion, London School of Economics (London), 2003.
8. Michael Rutter, 'Resilience as a Dynamic Concept', *Development and Psychopathology,* 24 (2), May 2012, pp 335–44.
9. Norman A Constantine, Bonnie Benard and Marycruz Diaz, 'Measuring Moderating Factors and Resilience Traits in Youth: The Healthy Kids Resilience Assessment', paper presented at the Seventh Annual Meeting of the Society for Prevention Research, New Orleans, 1999: https://pdfs.semanticscholar.org/53fe/3644fa36a4755485b9ad9b5b59ec9de08eff.pdf.
10. Nina Mguni and Nicola Bacon, *Taking the Temperature of Local Communities: The Wellbeing and Resilience Measure (WARM),* Young Foundation (London), 2010.
11. Adam Tinson *et al, London Poverty Profile,* Trust for London (London) 2017, p 10.
12. Bacon, Goodship and Naylor, *op cit,* 2019.
13. Understanding Society, 'The UK Household Longitudinal Study': www.understandingsociety.ac.uk/.
14. Trust for London, *'London's Poverty Profile':* www.trustforlondon.org.uk/data/.
15. Larry Gonick and Woollcott Smith, *The Cartoon Guide to Statistics,* HarperCollins (New York), 1993, P 213.
16. *Ibid,* p 212.
17. Office for National Statistics, '2011 Residential-based Area Classifications': www.ons.gov.uk/methodology/geography/geographicalproducts/areaclassifications/2011areaclassifications.
18. Ministry of Housing, Communities & Local Government, 'English Indices of Deprivation 2015', 30 September 2015: www.gov.uk/government/statistics/english-indices-of-deprivation-2015.

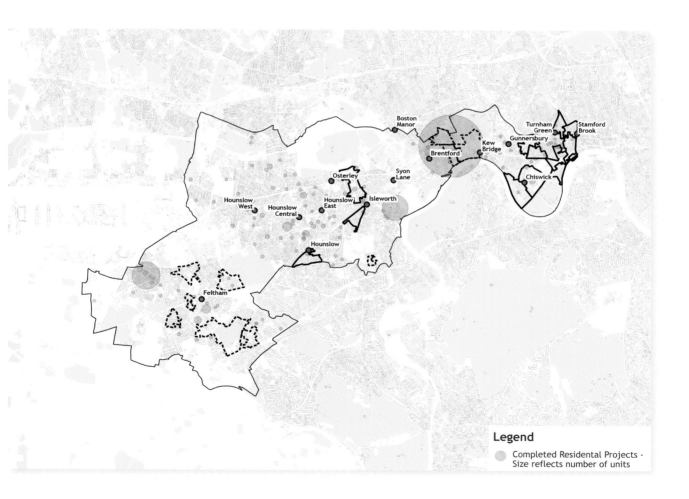

Legend

● Completed Residental Projects - Size reflects number of units

GREEN KEEPER

ESTABLISHING THE FULL VALUE OF GREEN

We know that exposure to green space can make us happier, but how do we qualify its benefits? **Jenni Montgomery**, business development director at planning and design consultancy Barton Willmore, explains the practice's co-creation of Greenkeeper, a data-driven software tool that makes visual the use and specific societal advantages of existing green space, but also can be used projectively to posit new green spaces in urban areas.

Evaluating success is challenging, no matter what sphere you are operating within. Demonstrating economic value is often simplest, but in the development industry, finding ways to understand and quantify environmental and societal benefit is increasingly critical in illustrating the long-term success of projects. Looking more specifically at green infrastructure, this challenge intensifies in urban areas. Barton Willmore's planners and designers deliver city regeneration and intensification UK-wide and frequently challenge what is widely regarded as outdated, standards-based green-space policy. But what if we could better evaluate the benefit we know green delivers to support and enhance this debate?

Greenkeeper,
Green space benefits,
2019

The Greenkeeper team used this diagram in the earliest stages of development to articulate the key benefits that green space delivers for communities, seeking to ensure the online tool can quantify these and therefore provide a measure of both social and economic value.

To date, methods for evaluating green infrastructure have largely been delivered by the economic or academic sectors. Vivid Economics, for example, is a strategic consultancy looking to use economics to support commercial decision-making, and a leader in the development of Natural Capital Accounts for London,[1] while the University of Exeter's European Centre for Environment & Human Health (ECEHH) developed the Outdoor Recreational Valuation tool (ORVal)[2] online platform in 2016, which used travel costs to value nature. Both are great approaches, but their complexity and a lack of accessibility for non-specialist users means they have not, thus far, been adopted more broadly by the public or private property industries. What if a tool could be developed that applies leading econometrics and academic research in this field to a mainstream online platform, designed to reflect and fit within the planning and development process?

In late 2017, Barton Willmore, Vivid Economics and the ECEHH therefore approached Innovate UK to secure funding for the development of Greenkeeper, a data-driven model and easy-to-use online application that can level the playing field for local authorities, designers, developers and communities alike by driving understanding of urban green-space value and how it may be enhanced for the benefit of all. Focused on supporting research and development, Innovate UK looks to support collaboration that creates competitive advantage for UK businesses. Any projects it supports must deliver commercially viable, marketable outputs within its tightly established time, budget and reporting structures. Quickly overcoming approach and language challenges inherent within the unusually diverse Greenkeeper collaboration was therefore imperative.

Greenkeeper combines findings from Natural England's Monitor of Engagement with the Natural Environment (MENE) (of 45,000 people a year) with demographic information and mobile phone location data to build a picture of who uses green space, their length of stay, frequency and activity levels, from which it can calculate a comprehensive estimate of visitor numbers. It then utilises monetary values based on emerging quality-adjusted life year (QALY) and wellbeing ECEHH methodologies to calculate the physical health and wellbeing value for visitors, as well as enhancements for neighbouring properties (house price/property uplift) and the value derived from carbon sequestration (identified tree canopy cover assessed and the level of carbon reduction the trees can deliver, monetised using untraded carbon statistics).

As such, it provides a social, economic and environmental value for the green space, expressed in monetary terms. Users of the app can therefore understand performance and identify potential improvements via a simple assessment and benchmarking interface. The powerful model driving the app can also be used offline, by the consultancy team, to measure the potential social value of specific interventions and, importantly, the creation of new green spaces for the purpose of informing design briefs, proposal testing, pre-application discussions, community engagement, funding and management decisions.

The powerful model driving the app can also be used offline, by the consultancy team, to measure the potential social value of specific interventions

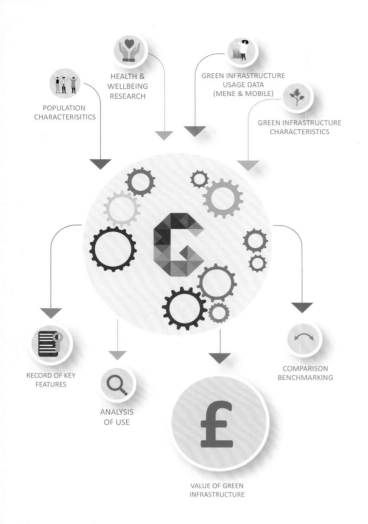

POPULATION
CHARACTERISITICS

HEALTH &
WELLBEING
RESEARCH

GREEN INFRASTRUCTURE
USAGE DATA
(MENE & MOBILE)

GREEN INFRASTRUCTURE
CHARACTERISTICS

RECORD OF KEY
FEATURES

ANALYSIS
OF USE

VALUE OF GREEN
INFRASTRUCTURE

COMPARISON
BENCHMARKING

Recent research by Exeter University shows that regardless of what you do in a green space, exposure to it is associated with higher levels of life satisfaction for every visitor

Greenkeeper model,
2019

The Greenkeeper online app collates physical, demographic and usage data layers for over 20,000 green spaces across England and Scotland. The Greenkeeper model then analyses this information alongside emerging health benefits research. Once processed through the model, the application will output an annual visitor estimate and associated values from an economic, social and environmental perspective.

Greenkeeper app,
2019

The Greenkeeper app has been designed to offer users a simple interface through which to select and analyse urban green spaces in towns and cities across England and Scotland. Once a space has been selected, mapped data layers provide access to demographic and physical information, a predicted annual visits number based on this information, and a resultant value breakdown. The values can then be benchmarked against other green spaces of a similar scale.

Example: quantifying the value of Crossway Park
£1 spent on maintenance provides £24 in benefits

GREEN IS GOOD FOR YOU

During the development of the tool, two findings stood out as being key to understanding the social value of green. Firstly, through analysis of visitor patterns, it is evident that close to 90 per cent of visitors to green space are 'active', be this to a moderate (walking a dog) or high (going for a run/cycle) level. Physical health benefits are derived for all these individuals and are valued in Greenkeeper using the UK Government's guidance on QALYs or 'value of a statistical life'.[3] Clearly, those who are regularly active derive far greater value, specifically reducing their risk of ischaemic heart disease, stroke and Type 2 diabetes, and design interventions that encourage and facilitate more people to make active green-space visits will therefore lead to a significant increase in social value for a community.

The second finding is focused on the lesser-understood or -quantified benefits to wellbeing, defined as 'general life satisfaction'. Recent research by Exeter University shows that regardless of what you do in a green space, exposure to it is associated with higher levels of life satisfaction for every visitor.[4] What is particularly interesting is the importance of 'dose'. Individuals gain incremental benefits from increasing doses of green immersion, but this benefit in wellbeing plateaus quite significantly at around 120 minutes per week. Interventions that increase the chance of any individual gaining 120 minutes' immersion in green spaces per week will therefore assist in securing maximum wellbeing benefits for the highest proportion of our towns or cities.

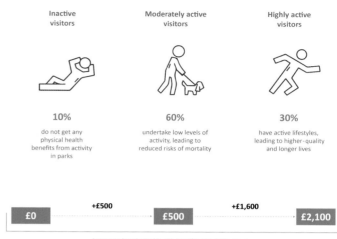

Average value physical health benefits per visitor per year

Greenkeeper,
Activity classifications and resultant derived value,
2019

People use green spaces for different purposes. Having compared anonymised mobile phone location information with the Natural England Monitor of Engagement with the Natural Environment (MENE) green-space visitor data, the Greenkeeper team was able to build a view of the proportion of visitors within three distinct activity level groups: in UK parks the team has found that, on average, 10 per cent of visitors are inactive, 60 per cent moderately active, and 30 per cent highly active. The physical health value each of these groups derives per annum differs due to their activity level during the visit. Using the new health benefits methodology devised by the University of Exeter's European Centre for Environment & Human Health (ECEHH), the team is able to attribute a monetary value to this, per visitor, per annum.

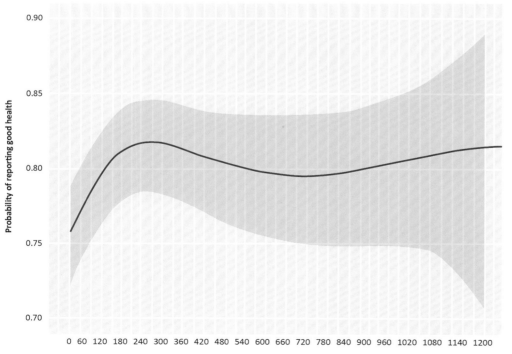

European Centre for Environment & Human Health (ECEHH),
Probability of Reporting Good Health,
2019

Research led by the ECEHH established a methodology for understanding the wellbeing benefits derived by visitors to green space. The graph charts the probability of an individual reporting 'good health' against the length of time spent in green space per week, and shows that an optimum wellbeing benefit is secured at around 120 minutes, beyond which the 'value' secured plateaus.

Barton Willmore,
Rdg2050: Vision for Reading 2050,
Reading, England,
2017

right: Illustration demonstrating the potential of 'greening' Reading's current inner distribution road. Barton Willmore's vision sets out ambitions to enhance green infrastructure provision and connectivity throughout the town through the enhancement of existing green spaces and creating new ones.

below: Reading's rivers can also enhance green connectivity. A city of rivers and parks should celebrate its waterways, opening them up as green and blue corridors of movement, but also as the focus for the town's cultural and leisure activities.

CHANGING THE WAY WE DESIGN

Over the past five years, Barton Willmore has been working closely with the town of Reading to develop an ambitious Vision for 2050[5] that can deliver enhanced quality of life for all residents. The town has an extensive existing network of rivers and parks that are believed to be largely underutilised and ignored. It is also facing a significant degree of urban intensification in the coming years.

Through the Greenkeeper app and wider model, Barton Willmore planners and designers have begun to assess and benchmark the town's green spaces. Understanding how the portfolio, across its breadth, performs different functions, and which of the town's diverse communities can and are actively using these spaces, can help to shape the top-level policy moves needed to enhance provision. But most interestingly, Greenkeeper analyses can inform what short and medium-term incremental steps might enable the town to secure the longer-term ambitions outlined in the 2050 vision, such as 'greening' the inner distribution road (IDR) and opening up the River Kennet to greater cultural and recreational uses.

In terms of Reading's ambition to 'close the gap' between deprived and economically successful communities, Greenkeeper can identify which local areas are struggling to access green space and therefore missing out on the resultant health benefits. It can inform interventions to facilitate the 120-minute immersion target by connecting green spaces, making these benefits tangible for all and embedding them in daily activities and commutes in a town wishing to better celebrate its rivers and parks. It can also inform how we design streetscapes and gardens, parks and riversides as well as the buildings fronting on to them, to maximise the value derived.

Although currently only developed using geographic and green-space usage data from England and Scotland, the Greenkeeper model and approach is already being picked up internationally, and the team is therefore considering how it can be adapted to reflect cultural variances in Europe and beyond. It is also looking at how functionality can be enhanced to enable interventions and new-space assessments directly through the app, as well as analyses of the value of tree-lined streets and water bodies, to broaden the opportunities for embedding the tool in the design and management process from beginning to end. ⌀

Notes

1. Robin Smale *et al*, *Natural Capital Accounts for Public Green Space in London*, October 2017: www.london.gov.uk/sites/default/files/11015viv_natural_capital_account_for_london_v7_full_vis.pdf.
2. www.exeter.ac.uk/leep/research/orval/.
3. HM Treasury, *The Green Book: Central Government Guidance on Appraisal and Valuation*, 2018, p 73: https://assets.publishing.service.gov.uk/government/uploads/system/uploads/attachment_data/file/685903/The_Green_Book.pdf.
4. Mathew White *et al*, 'Spending at Least 120 Minutes a Week in Nature is associated with Good Health and Wellbeing', *Scientific Reports*, 9(1), 7730, 2019: https://ore.exeter.ac.uk/repository/handle/10871/37706.
5. Jenni Montgomery *et al*, *Rdg 2050: A Vision for Reading 2050*, 2017: https://livingreading.co.uk/reading-2050.

High Science and Low Technology for Sustainable Rural Development

Li Wan and Edward Ng

Houses of Guangming village,
Yunnan province, China,
after the earthquake,
2014

Most of the traditional rammed-earth
houses were seriously damaged by
the earthquake.

Is it possible to mitigate the poor housing, poor safety and lack of dignity of the population in vast areas of rural China without adding to the environmental load? Co-founders of the One University One Village initiative **Li Wan and Edward Ng,** of the School of Architecture at the Chinese University of Hong Kong, believe that it is, and describe their activities to this end in these regions.

'Architecture is a tool to improve lives.'

— Anna Heringer [1]

Daily life in poor rural areas of China can be quite different from that in urban areas. There are 14 contiguous destitute areas in China.[2] Children in these areas may face challenges such as living in mountain villages with poor transportation and little access to education. The agricultural income of families is low due to poor environmental conditions and frequent natural disasters. Old houses, which were built decades ago using local natural materials and manpower, have become uncomfortable and unsafe to live in. Residents' only hope is to rebuild their houses using brick, steel and concrete that need to be brought from other locations and transported into the village. To earn enough money to pay for construction materials and hire a construction team, parents have to leave their homes to become migrant workers in cities. Hence, children are left alone with their grandparents. Eventually, these children develop the same desire to leave the village when they grow up.

China has a vast territory and a large population of 1.39 billion. Rural construction and development is a key issue in China – as of 2017, 41.48 per cent of the population were living in rural areas.[3] Under a series of top-down rural support and development policies since 2005, the government has increased funding for rural infrastructure, such as roads, irrigation, water supply systems, power supply systems, communication systems and biogas.[4] The country's rural areas have been subjected to rapid development and construction. In those which have relatively convenient transportation, the modernisation development model has significantly improved quality of life and urban–rural integration.[5]

Conventional new buildings, which use industrial materials, are usually unaffordable to poor rural residents. Even when people borrow money to improve their buildings, the quality and performance remain unsatisfactory because of unfamiliarity with modern design and construction practices. A large amount of rural construction with industrial materials can lead to a sharp increase in energy consumption and consequent environmental load. Moreover, top-down planning and construction, which often lack public engagement and consideration of the actual needs of villagers, have led to a reduction of cultural identity and sense of belonging.[6]

Xuefeng He, an expert on rural policy and management, has observed that large-scale, mechanised cultivation is unsuitable for poor rural areas, especially mountainous ones, where land is divided into small pieces. Most rural residents who work in urban areas still want to return to their rural hometowns upon reaching old age because urban areas cannot provide a decent life for them, given the current level of urban development. Chinese rural development needs to provide economic and social support to small-scale peasant economies and aged farmers. He also argued that the aim of Chinese sustainable rural development should be to provide a proper rural living environment, where most rural residents can live a decent life, rather than bringing rural residents' standard of living up to urban levels.[7]

Influenced by rural development at home and abroad, in 2013 the Chinese government proposed the construction of The Beautiful Countryside, which stressed the value of the natural environment and local culture.[8] In 2015, China's State Council launched a series of specific poverty alleviation strategies, which consider environmental prevention, local resident empowerment and endogenous development.[9] In this way, the rural development model has become increasingly diversified and humanised.

The Significance of Socioeconomic Value in Rural Development

Research has shown that socioeconomic value is crucial in sustainable rural construction and development. In most poor rural areas, including the 14 contiguous destitute areas mentioned above, the main problem is not high energy consumption and carbon emission, as the environmental load of traditional houses built using local natural materials and manpower is low. The real problem is how to improve the safety, quality and dignity of the living environment without adding substantial environmental load. Raising hundreds of millions of people's standard of living can lead to a considerable environmental load if the wrong strategy is adopted.

Relying on external funds, non-local industrial materials and high technologies can cause huge environmental risks to poor rural areas. It is unrealistic for rural residents to stay in their village and contribute to the local development if they have no confidence in their local resources, lifestyles and abilities. Even if a new farmhouse can be built with external funds and support, villagers will still try to get rid of everything 'local', which in their mind represents poverty. Only by endogenous development which values local resources, local technologies and local culture can villagers see a bright future for their homes.

Choosing appropriate building materials, building technologies and construction workers is crucial and tricky in poor rural areas. While the architectural form and total construction cost is important, the architect must also consider bioclimatic design, the proportion of material costs to labour costs, the source of materials and workers (an important aspect of social value) and the operability of building technology.

Practice and Experience from Guangming Village

Guangming village is located in a mountainous region in Yunnan province – one of China's 14 contiguous destitute areas. Most of its houses were built decades ago out of rammed earth. Indoor spaces were dark and poorly ventilated because of the limited building height and window openings that this traditional construction method entails. When a 6.1-magnitude earthquake seriously damaged 90 per cent of these buildings in August 2014, the villagers lost confidence in them.

Similarly to most rural residents, the Guangming villagers needed to make a choice between local vernacular and modern brick-concrete building methods during the post-earthquake reconstruction. Most chose the latter, even though it was expensive. The reason behind this was a lack of knowledge and motivation to innovate amongst the local craftsmen because a substantial number of them had chosen to become migrant workers in urban areas. The urban lifestyle has influenced people's views of vernacular architecture. Most rural residents thought that earthen buildings indicated poverty. Moreover, high-speed top-down rural construction built with external capital has limited the time and space available for innovation with local traditional methods.

The post-earthquake reconstruction project in Guangming village was developed in response to this situation. Its aim was to improve upon the traditional rammed-earth building method to provide a safe, economical, comfortable and sustainable reconstruction system which the villagers can afford, own and pass on, and which focuses on seismic capacity, thermal comfort and cost-effectiveness. It was organised by the One University One Village (1U1V) rural programme of the Chinese University of Hong Kong (CUHK), which was financed by the Chan Cheung Mun Chung Charitable Fund. The project was supported by Kunming University of Science and Technology (KUST) and the University of Cambridge in terms of seismic performance improvement.

To achieve systematic and sustainable rural reconstruction work with innovative ideas, scientific research is essential in order to understand the context and identify the problem. On the basis of a literature review of earthen building technology[10] and a study of weak points of local traditional rammed-earth houses, several innovations including building structure optimisation, soil composition optimisation, and construction tools improvement were proposed to improve seismic performance. A series of mechanical property tests and shaking table tests were conducted to validate the innovative technology. Results reveal that the seismic performance of the new rammed-earth building has significantly improved, thus fulfilling the local seismic codes perfectly.

To promote endogenous development and empower residents, a prototype house was designed for an elderly couple based on all the research and testing that had gone before. It was then built by locals, between December 2015 and April 2016. Villagers can learn about the new technology, understand the construction costs, and appreciate the building quality directly, by themselves. Basic human needs, such as safety and comfort, are highlighted in the project to allow the residents to feel cared for and respected. Locals then become more willing to try to participate in the testing and training. Furthermore, they can easily feel and understand the benefit of the innovative technology after the completion of the demonstration project. This process is essential for the villagers to accept the innovative technology.

The architectural design of the house has also been carefully considered to fit the rural lifestyle. Bioclimatic design with recycled materials gathered from local ruins can ensure high building performance and low environmental load. The semi-outdoor atrium can provide a comfortable and artistic living environment for the couple, with a skylight and cross-ventilation. In addition to the thermal mass of the thick earthen wall, the double-glazed windows and insulated roofs further improved the building's thermal performance. Multifunctional spaces in the upper floor, which can be used

Edward Ng, Li Wan, Xinan Chi and Wenfeng Bai,
Prototype house for Guangming village
post-earthquake reconstruction,
The Chinese University of Hong Kong and
Kunming University of Science and Technology,
2016

All architectural elements were properly designed, thereby resulting in a natural and desirable atmosphere in harmony with the surrounding environment and the local cultural heritage. Contrasting with the brick house next to it, this house allows the villagers to recall the traditional construction system and local culture.

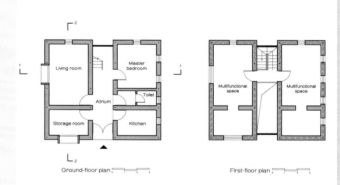

Ground-floor plan

First-floor plan

The building is integrated with semi-outdoor spaces to provide a comfortable and artistic living environment for the resident elderly couple, Mr and Mrs Yang. Its design is simple and easy to implement based on the current technology and the ability of villagers.

Section 1

Section 2

The semi-outdoor atrium has natural cross-ventilation and a skylight for daylighting. Double-glazed windows and insulated roofs were used to improve the building's thermal performance. A steel roof structure and aluminium alloy windows were employed to increase building quality and airtightness.

as storage rooms, guest rooms or workplaces, have been provided to adapt to the villagers' agricultural production activities and rural lifestyles. Again, the building design is simple, and can be easily understood and implemented on the basis of villagers' existing knowledge and ability.

Local Material, Local Technology, Local Labour

The response to the specific historical context of Guangming village has not been to imitate the form of the local traditional buildings but to regenerate local culture by following the principle of '3L': local material, local technology and local labour. It attempts to rekindle the endogenous vitality of traditional architecture rather than maintain the appearance of traditional architecture without consideration of residents' new physical and social needs. Instead of promoting the benefits of imported bricks and concrete, the project team addressed the shortfalls of traditional rammed-earth technology and the fragility of village life in situ. The easiest way to teach the technology to villagers is to innovate on the basis of the technology they are already familiar with. It is the '3L' principle that makes the project not only 'a project in the village', but more importantly, 'a project for villagers'.

The use of natural and recycled materials from seismic ruins has minimised construction costs. The cost of the prototype houses was only approximately 60 per cent of that of a local conventional brick-concrete building. Unlike the brick-concrete building, where the materials are costly but less is spent on labour, these two types of cost for the prototype houses were balanced at roughly half-and-half, which means that this type of rammed-earth building values human labour and unique local skills rather than building materials.

Villagers who were trained and employed to build houses were able to use these skills to make a living. For example, the construction team leader, Mr Yang, had sworn that he would never build earth houses again because his wife had been killed by a collapsing earth house during the earthquake. After learning about the research, testing and design of the 1U1V team, he volunteered to be the leader of the construction team for his parents' house because he used to be a construction worker. His confidence in the innovative rammed-earth building method grew as the construction progressed, and as the project eventually won several international awards including World Building of the Year Award at the World Architecture Festival 2017, an *Architectural Review* (AR) House Award in 2017 and a Grand Award in the Hong Kong Green Building Awards 2019. After the tragedy of the earthquake, Mr Yang and his family regained a decent life and confidence in the future. Nowadays, he can pay for his children's tuition fees and support his elderly parents using his earnings from construction work in surrounding villages. Such success stories have proved the high social and economic value of this 'high-science and low-technology' strategy with the 3L principle.

Edward Ng, Li Wan, Xinan Chi and Wenfeng Bai, Prototype house for Guangming village post-earthquake reconstruction, The Chinese University of Hong Kong and Kunming University of Science and Technology, 2016

Multifunctional spaces that can be used as storage rooms, guest rooms or workplaces have been provided to adapt to the villagers' lifestyles. The result has convinced many local government officers and residents that rammed-earth houses can be safe, clean, comfortable and beautiful.

The semi-outdoor atrium is bright and comfortable. Mrs Yang can devote more of her time to embroidery.

The easiest way to teach the technology to villagers is to innovate on the basis of the technology they are already familiar with

Edward Ng, Li Wan,
Xinan Chi and
Wenfeng Bai,
Prototype house for
Guangming village
post-earthquake
reconstruction,
The Chinese University
of Hong Kong and
Kunming University
of Science
and Technology,
2016

right: All construction team
members were local villagers.
An electric rammer was used,
along with aluminium alloy
formwork instead of wood, to
make the wall very compact and
smooth. The technology is easy for
villagers to learn and operate.

below: Householders Mr and
Mrs Yang in front of the prototype
house. After the earthquake, they
thought they would have to live
in a tent for the rest of their lives.
Fortunately, this project allows
them to regain the dignity of
living. They feel very proud of their
house when people visit and give
positive comments.

Architects, builders and owners discussing in the village. An architect lived on site in the village to guide the construction work and ensure its quality. A strong relationship of trust between the project team and the villagers was established.

Allowing the Villagers to Become the Owners

Rural construction is not a one-way output from architects to villagers, but a mutually beneficial process. In the Guangming village post-earthquake reconstruction project, multidisciplinary university resources, which include architecture, civil engineering and earthquake engineering, are fully supportive of rural reconstruction. The initiative has provided the project team with valuable research resources and local experience that were unavailable to them in the ivory tower. They contribute to scientific research and on-site guidance, with residents providing the local experience and manpower. The project team has learned just as much from the experience as the villagers have; if the effort from either side had been lacking, it would not have been a successful venture. A relationship of trust between the project team and villagers was established during the construction process – a collective form of social value.

Since the construction of the prototype, 17 more village houses have been rebuilt using this innovated rammed-earth building method in Yunnan and Sichuan provinces. More than 70 houses are now under construction. The benefits in terms of social, economic and environmental value have been immense.

China's architects have been involved in more and more rural improvement projects over the last 10 years, but most of them are not prepared for this task, as they have so little experience of rural life. If architects want to use architecture as a tool to improve lives in rural areas, as Anna Heringer – a German architect who was famous for designing the METI Handmade School in Bangladesh – has argued, and if they want to improve the social-economic value of rural areas, the first step is to stand in the villagers' shoes. In many ways the environment and culture of rural areas is more varied and complex than in urban ones, which have been influenced by globalisation. Architects need to learn to integrate into rural life and find the opportunities within local development, rather than impose strategies from outside that are inappropriate to the setting. The only way to improve social-economic value in rural construction is to allow the villagers to become the masters of their buildings and their lives. ⌂

Notes
1. 'Vision': www.anna-heringer.com/.
2. Yuan Tian, Zheng Wang, Jincai Zhao, Xuan Jiang and Rongxing Guo, 'A Geographical Analysis of the Poverty Causes in China's Contiguous Destitute Areas', *Sustainability*, 10 (6), 2018, p 1895.
3. National Bureau of Statistics of China, *China Statistical Yearbook 2018*, China Statistics Press (Beijing), 2018: www.stats.gov.cn/tjsj/ndsj/2018/indexeh.htm.
4. Xianghu Lu, 'A Retrospect of "No 1 Document" and its Corresponding Enlightenments for Implementing the Strategy of Rural Vitalization' (in Chinese), *Journal of Chongqing Jiaotong University (Social Sciences Edition)*, 19, 2019, pp 6–11.
5. Yichi Zhang and Ruixi Dai, 'Influence of Rural Infrastructure on the Economic Growth of Agriculture: An Empirical Analysis Based on the National Provincial Panel Data' (in Chinese), *Journal of Agrotechnical Economics*, 3, 2018, pp 90–99.
6. Chaoying Zhang, Chenxia Suo and Wei Deng Solvang, *Efficiency and Effectiveness of Energy-efficient Building Technology in Chinese Rural Area* (in Chinese), Economic Science Press (Beijing), 2010, pp 36–9; 'Planning and Construction of Villages and Towns in the Age of Ecological Civilization' (in Chinese): www.mohurd.gov.cn/jsbfld/200903/t20090316_187287.html.
7. Xuefeng He, 'Agricultural Modernization for Whom?' (in Chinese), *Open Times*, 2015, pp 36–48.
8. Qiuhong Chen and Fawen Yu, 'A Review of the Research and Practice of the Beautiful Countryside Construction' (in Chinese), *Study and Practice*, 6, 2014, pp 107–16.
9. 'Decision of the CPC Central Committee and the State Council on Winning the Tough Battle against Poverty' (in Chinese): http://news.xinhuanet.com/politics/2015-12/07/c_1117383987.htm.
10. Hugo Houben and Hubert Guillard, *Earth Construction: A Comprehensive Guide*, Intermediate Technology Publications (London), 1994, pp 73–106.

Architecture from the Ground Up

Designing and Delivering Social Value in Southern India

Architect **Jateen Lad** details the socially empowering design and project delivery strategies for the Sharanam Centre for Rural Development in southern India and their catalytic effect on local communities. The trust and dialogue between the architect, NGO client and workers was crucial in the development of technical skills and improved livelihoods that continue to help the communities thrive.

Jateen Lad,
Sharanam Centre for Rural Development,
near Pondicherry, India,
2016

The interior is integrated with nature and filled with fresh air. The main hall is defined by a large granite *thinnai* detailed with dry joints and scaled for an audience of 200, interactive workshops for 50 to 60, small group meetings and niches for personal space.

Built at the edge of a rural landscape destroyed by illegal quarrying, the Sharanam Centre for Rural Development (2016) enables SARVAM (Sri Aurobindo Rural Village Action and Movement), a local NGO, to expand its transformation of chronically impoverished villages outside Pondicherry in southern India. Meaning 'refuge', Sharanam hosts local communities in programmes covering all aspects of rural life including health, education, self-development and poverty alleviation.

The design and delivery of the project was structured to generate social value through a hands-on approach far removed from conventional practice. Social value, in this context, was defined in four ways: as enriching a project brief to address pressing local concerns through architecture; as the design of a place of beauty, wellbeing and respect for those ordinarily denied access to such environments; as instilling shared ethical and cultural values into the management of the project; and as maximising community involvement in the process.

Early-Stage Research

The strength of Sharanam's social value lies in early-stage research. With no firm brief, funding or site, it became necessary to shadow SARVAM's outreach work with local communities mired in acute poverty and bottom of the scale in education, health and sanitation. Alcoholism, violence and domestic abuse were endemic. A resistance to change – what SARVAM described as a 'heavy inertia' – was deeply entrenched. A scarcity of jobs compounded the poverty of aspiration. Generational skills, particularly in traditional building trades, were lost to an unregulated construction boom dependent upon cement and cheap migrant labour expected to work all hours and live in squalor on site. The damage to a once healthy rural environment has been apocalyptic.

The challenge was to connect these heavily loaded findings into workable design, procurement and practice strategies to generate social value. Testing possibilities with user groups and social pioneers enabled the development of an overall brief: to create a stimulating building by employing local people and local resources in an ethical and socially empowering manner.

To assist the client to get the project off the ground, effective fundraising assets were generated. A compelling visual narrative, grounded in research, was pitched to potential donors. This helped secure a long-term funding partnership with the Cadbury Foundation supporting full project costs and the acquisition of a 2-hectare (5-acre) site accessible to the wider rural district.

Jateen Lad,
Sharanam Centre for Rural Development,
near Pondicherry, India,
2016

left: Local NGO SARVAM (Sri Aurobindo Rural Village Action and Movement) initiated its pioneering rural development programmes from a small thatched-roof pavilion. By mid-2007, a new purpose-designed campus was proposed to broaden the organisation's reach.

Hand-built from the earth of the site, this bespoke building enables SARVAM to expand its development reach across the district. With no contractor, architect Jateen Lad managed the construction to provide employment and to upgrade the skills of over 300 local workers.

Designing for Social Value

The spread of illegal quarrying had rendered large areas of the site ecologically barren. However, with careful plantation and ethical construction practices, the long-abused landscape was dramatically revived, creating a place of beauty, wellbeing and respect for the poorest of the rural poor.

Sharanam comprises a large vaulted multipurpose hall, meeting spaces, offices, a newspaper studio, radio station, community kitchen and infrastructure integrated with nature. The buildings are constructed from the most local of resources, the red soil of the site, from which 200,000 unfired earth blocks were manually pressed. This minimised cement usage and the embodied carbon of the fabric. The superstructure comprises an array of thin masonry vaults spanning an uplifting interior balancing multipurpose community spaces with secluded verandas perched over ponds and under trees. The main hall, proportioned to the golden ratio, is defined by a massive granite *thinnai* – the raised multi-use platform of traditional Tamil homes – designed for small meetings, workshops and performances. A smaller circular hall is set out under the detached eastern vault, while folding walls playfully conceal and slowly reveal private courtyards and offices.

In a hot tropical climate, social spaces remain ineffective without environmental comfort. The piers funnel fresh breezes into the building. Embedded cooling pipes and cool-to-touch finishes ensure thermal comfort without air-conditioning, while maturing trees and earthen tones soften the harsh light. Interiors step out on to generous verandas that merge into gardens with soft ground cover and scented flowering trees.

An entrance sequence defined by water leads through eucalyptus groves, gardens and an existing avenue of palmyra trees. A shaded green amphitheatre cut into the natural slope of the site acts as a place of welcome.

Key
1. Entrance avenue
2. Green amphitheatre
3. Entrance ponds
4. Reception
5. Vestibule
6. Multipurpose hall
7. Granite *thinnai* and stage
8. Vault pond
9. Circular hall
10. North verandas and garden terraces
11. South verandas and courtyard
12. Administrative office with roof garden
13. Meeting space
14. Newspaper studio with gallery above
15. Store with roof garden
16. Research office with roof garden
17. Rainwater sump
18. Excavation pit/reservoir

Axonometric of the main building interior showing the arrangement of community gathering spaces, private offices and secluded verandas merging with the gardens and landscape.

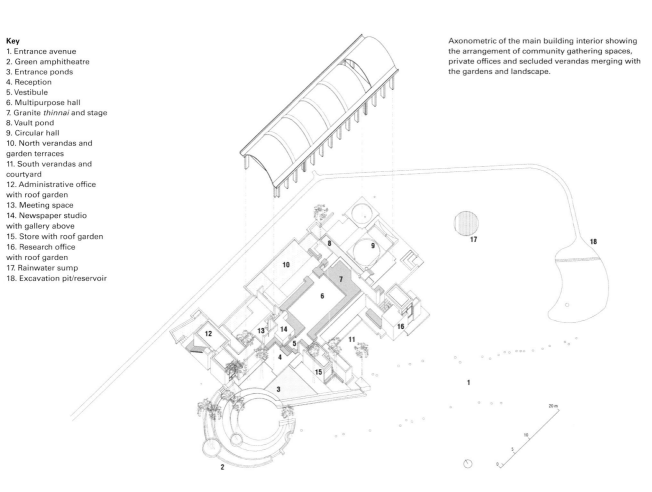

Instilling Shared Ethical and Cultural Values

Client-architect relationships built on trust and openness allow certain risk-taking. With shared concerns over the local construction industry, a wider scope of service was required. Cost management provided transparency and accountability to funders. Bribes, unaccounted commissions and tax avoidance were cut out. Full construction management controlled quality and ensured that ethical practices, on and off site, were upheld. Direct procurement of materials allowed inspections of supply chains, down to quarries and saw mills, for environmental standards and evidence of bonded or child labour.

This holistic approach accommodated the community in the process to generate social value. User groups were encouraged to participate in placemaking exercises. Early discussions over sketches reinforced the *thinnai* as the primary cultural element. Sensitive cultural practices were absorbed into detailing, for example when and where to remove footwear articulated materiality, thresholds and level changes across the entire floorplate.

Elsewhere, co-design sessions for the kitchen and toilets aimed to improve poor sanitation and hygiene standards. Both facilities were not consigned to back-of-house areas, but developed as spacious, freestanding buildings integrated with nature and flooded with natural light and fresh air. Bespoke detailing, durable materials and good plumbing prevent damage and flooding. To this day, both buildings, despite constant usage, are treated respectfully and remain spotlessly clean.

Generating Social Value through the Construction Process

The making of Sharanam, from top to bottom, was programmed as its own development project. Construction funds were not only used to make buildings, but invested into long-term livelihoods to generate social value rather than apportioned for profit. With no contractor and a rudimentary toolkit, over 300 local workers were employed and trained on the job in wide-ranging skills including rammed earth, manufacturing earth blocks, structural masonry, reinforcement fabrication, carpentry, stonework, plumbing and finishing techniques. Collaborations with tradesmen refined detailing, revived traditional lime work and developed innovative concreting, precasting and plastering techniques.

Humane working hours (eight hours a day) and a transparent payment system incentivised workers, who set their own pay consistent to market rates. Face-to-face instructions, dedicated supervision and step-by-step drawings fostered trust between architect and workers, resulting in careful workmanship, reduced errors and costs. Many forged a strong identity with Sharanam, photographing their accomplishments with pride and renewed self-confidence. Key workers remain as a full-time maintenance team, their enduring bonds, knowledge and deep care keeping operational costs low.

This collective act of learning and building has proven rewarding and transformative. Over 55 per cent of construction costs were invested into local communities. New skills offered improved long-term livelihoods.

Jateen Lad,
Sharanam Centre for Rural Development,
near Pondicherry, India,
2016

A split-level pond cuts through the building. The natural acoustics of the vault carry the gentle sound of the waterfall through the interior, enhancing the sense of tranquillity and wellbeing.

The making of Sharanam, from top to bottom, was programmed as its own development project. Construction funds were not only used to make buildings, but invested into long-term livelihoods to generate social value rather than apportioned for profit

Close collaboration between the architect, tradesmen and daily wage workers refined the detailing. The private offices are notable for the full-height windows and sliding doors in reclaimed teak, precast structural soffits, insulating roof gardens and cool-to-touch earth plasters and dual-tone pigmented flooring.

Today, previously inexperienced workers are employed as masons, masons have become contractors, while carpenters and stoneworkers are undertaking lucrative professional contracts.

Despite the emphasis on process, delivery within budget remains critical for organisations fully dependent upon donations. At Sharanam, the wider range of architectural services accrued higher fees, but resulted in a high-quality building delivering considerable social and environmental value at less than half the cost of a standard concrete building in the region. Clearly, this approach disproves the often-stated excuse for poor building that 'good design costs money'.

Towards a New Practice

SARVAM's landmark building has proven transformative, significantly expanding the organisation's profile and outreach from two to over 20 villages, improving education, health, female empowerment and poverty alleviation across the district. Data are being collected on its impact not only for organisational learning, but also as a tool to lever further funding, and include savings in welfare and healthcare costs and the benefits of educational attainment, incomes, and lives free from alcoholism and violence.

Sharanam demonstrates strategies by which architects can drive projects to generate social value for impoverished communities. From getting projects off the ground to empowering local people through construction, architects working from the bottom up can enrich projects with long-term social benefits in the most difficult contexts. This requires a different, more holistic and fearless approach to practice connecting humane and empathetic design with research, social and environmental activism, collaborative building, financing and managing site operations. At a moment when the profession faces multiple challenges, the Sharanam project demonstrates how such an approach can enable architects to create something out of nothing to support local communities – and deliver high-quality, socially relevant buildings in the process.

Today, the narrative of Sharanam's socially empowering construction, now bolstered by social value data, attracts potential funders of future projects keen to learn from the process. However, the question remains to what extent social value goals will be compromised or even dispensed with during a project, particularly when programmes incur delays or costs escalate. Will clients and funders hold true to their commitments, allowing architects to pursue this new way of making architecture? ⌀

Workers with limited or no construction experience learnt a complete range of precision building skills. Masons, deskilled by a generation of infilling concrete frames, relearnt the basics of bonding, tolerance and pointing before being taught how to build large vaults through innovative self-supporting techniques.

Text © 2020 John Wiley & Sons Ltd. Images: pp 82–4, 85(t), 86–7 © Jateen Lad; p 85(b) © Jateen Lad, drawing by Alexandre Rossignol and Arianne Pizem

Cristina Garduño Freeman

In the Eye of the Beholder

Cristina Garduño Freeman,
Sails or Popcorn?,
2019

From the sublime to the ridiculous, the Sydney Opera House has prompted many analogies. 'Critiquing' might include 'seeing' the form of the building in sailing ships, shells and petals unfolding, or even in scattered popcorn or unrelated piles of washing up!

Is there a value in people's relationships with iconic buildings? **Cristina Garduño Freeman** argues there is – and that these social relationships can be identified and evaluated via digital ethnography. She illustrates her thesis using the Sydney Opera House and demonstrates how its 'iconomy' is a valuable social and economic asset.

Social value has always been a problem child for heritage. Unlike the other, more well-behaved values enshrined in the Australia International Council on Monuments and Sites (ICOMOS) Burra Charter,[1] such as historic, scientific and aesthetic value, social value is elusive and difficult to pin down. Yet we all have places, buildings and landscapes we feel connected to. These places hold our memories, enable social and cultural practices and articulate our identity. Social value is a present-day value held by individuals and communities, which means it cannot be 'evidenced' in buildings or the archives of their production. We have to look elsewhere to understand people's emotional connections with architecture.

An Icon: The Sydney Opera House

The clue to understanding how we can evidence social value lies in the idea of iconicity. Until now, iconic architecture has largely been framed as the materialisation of visionary design. Nowhere is this more obvious than for the Sydney Opera House, which is recognised by people all over the world; 8.2 million visitors each year and some 168 million connect with this place online.[2] It is a global icon, so much so that its status as a 'world famous iconic building'[3] was included as part of its outstanding universal value when it was designated a UNESCO World Heritage Site in 2007.

The Sydney Opera House was iconic before it was even built. Yet its discourse has focused on its architectural merit, technological innovation or the political events of its realisation. The story is punctuated by architect Jørn Utzon's resignation in 1966, seven years before its completion. Peter Hall, a young Australian architect, took the poisoned chalice

Cristina Garduño Freeman,
*Opera: The Eighth Wonder
and a Literary Genre,*
2019

opposite: From an aria to the saga, the story of the Sydney Opera House has an almost mythological status. In 'telling' the story of the building, people perform its realisation on blogs, with friends and for visitors.

and it opened in 1973.[4] This story has been told and revised so many times that it has even inspired an opera.[5] But such participation, from the popular to the scholarly, reveals how its iconicity is directly connected to its social value.

Iconicity is a Social Phenomenon

The Sydney Opera House, for example, was funded by the NSW State Lottery. Each £5 ticket featured an image of the building, with some 86.7 million sold during the years the lottery ran from 1957 to 1986. But these tickets were more than a simple wager for people. While their primary motivation was to win, they also participated because the money was going to a good cause.[6] Each ticket was an investment in this cultural place.

Using digital ethnography, social media and the Internet offer a window on to social value.[7] A simple search demonstrates how online references to the Sydney Opera

Jørn Utzon,
Competition drawing for the Sydney Opera House,
1956

Perspective sketch. Utzon always envisaged that the platform and staircases would elevate the spirit of the audience in preparation for the forthcoming performance. Little did he know that his sculptural proposal would gain worldwide recognition, cause controversy and prompt significant connections for people that are evident in popular culture.

Cristina Garduño Freeman,
An Icon Before it was Built,
2019

The construction of the Sydney Opera House (1973) was largely funded via the Opera House Lottery that opened in 1957 and ran until 1986. Each lottery ticket, like crowdfunding campaigns today, symbolised an investment by members of the public in the aspiration to build an opera house.

telling

Cristina Garduño Freeman,
Cap, Keyring and Stamp,
2019

By adding an image of the Sydney Opera House to everyday items such as caps, keyrings and stamps, individuals, groups and organisations are 'trading' on its cultural capital.

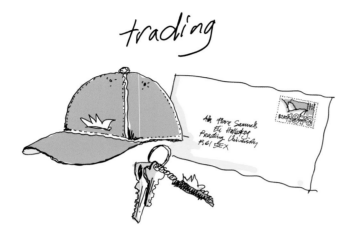

House are prolific. Art historian and critic Terry Smith describes this as the 'iconomy', a phenomenon where iconic places participate in the economy of cultural exchange.[8] Here, the image of the Sydney Opera House on a lottery ticket, a tourist snapshot posted to Flickr or Instagram, a kitsch snow globe purchased as a souvenir, or even an Opera House-inspired campervan become active agents of cultural capital by mediating the interactions between individuals and groups around a cultural locus that embodies a shared sense of identity.

After collecting and ordering over a thousand images of the Sydney Opera House,[9] analysis revealed that it is not the ephemera itself that is significant, but how it enables people to express their connections with the place. Interpreting the practices that both precede and follow such images exposes how people 'see' the building's iconic form in unrelated images: flowers unfolding; dishes in a dish rack; a dog's spikey hairdo; and even carefully arranged pieces of popcorn. Such subversive analogies 'critique' its discourses of sublime architecture. 'Telling' the story of the building's realisation is a way of appropriating the beginning of the place. Adding the Opera House to a mundane object like a pen or cap or on postage stamps and logos is 'trading' on its status. 'Capturing' the building in photographs structures how people move and engage with the architecture. Purchasing souvenirs is an attempt to turn the experience of 'visiting' into concrete memories. 'Making' an Opera House-shaped cake offers a role as an architect. Such connections with the place play on the tension between irreverent and respectful versions of this architectural masterpiece.[10]

Cristina Garduño Freeman,
Photographing the Sydney Opera House,
2019

The camera, the smartphone or the device enable the 'capturing' of the Opera House, a way of seeing, understanding and appreciating the building from every angle. Taking photos helps to structure people's physical experience into an accepted public ritual or performance.

Cristina Garduño Freeman,
Opera House Snowdome,
2019

Why do we collect kitsch souvenirs after 'visiting' the Sydney Opera House? A postcard or a miniature version of the building materialise and embody our desire to hold onto a special experience; their imperfection is no barrier to our memories.

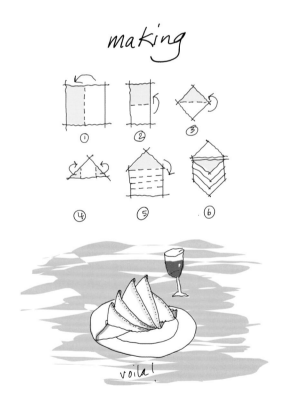

Cristina Garduño Freeman,
Opera Napkin Fold,
2019

'Making' the Sydney Opera House can be achieved in six easy steps. Take a napkin, fold it along the dotted lines and fold it again. Turn it 45 degrees and fold in half to form a triangle, then fold the points inwards. Finally, fold the leaves down one by one and voila, your table is adorned with miniature architectural masterpieces (also known as the Bird of Paradise napkin fold).

People Make Architecture Iconic

Audiences and communities have always been valuable social and economic assets, and the Internet now affords us more nuanced analysis. In 2018, Deloitte estimated the digital value of the Sydney Opera House at AU$166 million, but more impressive is their quantification of its iconic or 'existence value'. Measured through contingent valuation, Deloitte estimates this to be worth AU$2.2 billion.[11] Such figures are impressive measures of the building's social value. But they fail to describe it.

Iconicity and social value are relational; they exist in the social space located between buildings and people. Understood in this way, architecture, and heritage places, are 'quasi-objects'. Their social value lies in their ability to enable cultural practices, rather than as artefacts in an academic canon. This is not to say that their materiality is not significant, but rather to recognise that their social value is not solely evident in the building itself. Instead this pheonomenon allows for social significance to be networked across the related objects, practices and representations that exist beyond the site's boundaries and within the everyday lives of people.

Digital ethnography enables serious consideration of online social and visual practices. We can begin to understand who values buildings, how they value them, what these places mean, and when they are valued. Such an approach can be extended to places and buildings that may not be as spectacular as the Sydney Opera House, but may well be just as beloved. By looking first for evidence of emotional attachment, we can bring an open mind to understanding architecture from outside our profession and find ways to understand what makes places valuable to people. ∆

Notes
1. Australia ICOMOS, 'The Burra Charter: The Australia ICOMOS Charter for Places of Cultural Significance', 2013: http://australia. icomos.org/publications/charters/.
2. Sydney Opera House, *Sydney Opera House Annual Report 2015/16,* 2016: www.sydneyoperahouse.com/content/dam/pdfs/ annual-reports/Sydney_Opera_House_Annual_Report_2015-16.pdf.
3. 'Sydney Opera House (Australia) No 166 Rev: Advisory Body Evaluation', World Heritage Centre, 2007: http://whc.unesco.org/ archive/advisory_body_evaluation/166rev.pdf.
4. Anne Watson, *The Poisoned Chalice: Peter Hall and the Sydney Opera House,* OpusSOH Incorporated (Sydney), 2017.
5. Alan John and Dennis Watkins, *The Eighth Wonder,* Sydney Opera House, 1995.
6. Julie Power, 'New Australian Lottery Could Raise Funds for Heritage Projects', *Brisbane Times,* 8 December 2015: www. brisbanetimes.com.au/national/new-australian-lottery-could-raise-funds-for-heritage-projects-20151208-gli2jc.html.
7. Sarah Pink *et al, Digital Ethnography: Principles and Practice,* Sage (Los Angeles), 2016.
8. Terry Smith, 'The Political Economy of Iconotypes and the Architecture of Destination: Uluru, the Sydney Opera House and the World Trade Center', *Architectural Theory Review,* 7 (2), 2002, pp 1–43.
9. Dr Cristina Garduño Freeman, 2012: www.pinterest.com.au/ cristinagardunofreeman/.
10. Cristina Garduño Freeman, *Participatory Culture and the Social Value of an Architectural Icon: Sydney Opera House,* Routledge (Abingdon), 2018.
11. John O'Mahony *et al, Revaluing Our Icon: Midpoint in Sydney Opera House's Decade of Renewal,* Deloitte (Sydney), 2018, p 20: www.sydneyoperahouse.com/content/dam/pdfs/deloitte/ Deloitte%20Report_Revaluing%20Our%20Icon%202018.pdf.

**Aoibheann Ní Mhearáin
and Tara Kennedy**

Reframing Social Value in 20th-Century Conservation

Peter and Mary Doyle Architects,
St Brendan's Community School,
Birr, County Offaly, Ireland,
1979

This planometric featured in the publication of the newly built school in the
Architects' Journal in December 1980, and shows the sequential assembly of
the building. By illustrating it this way, the architects prioritised the building
process over its finished form, emphasising the system-based approach to
construction and the flexibility inherent in the design.

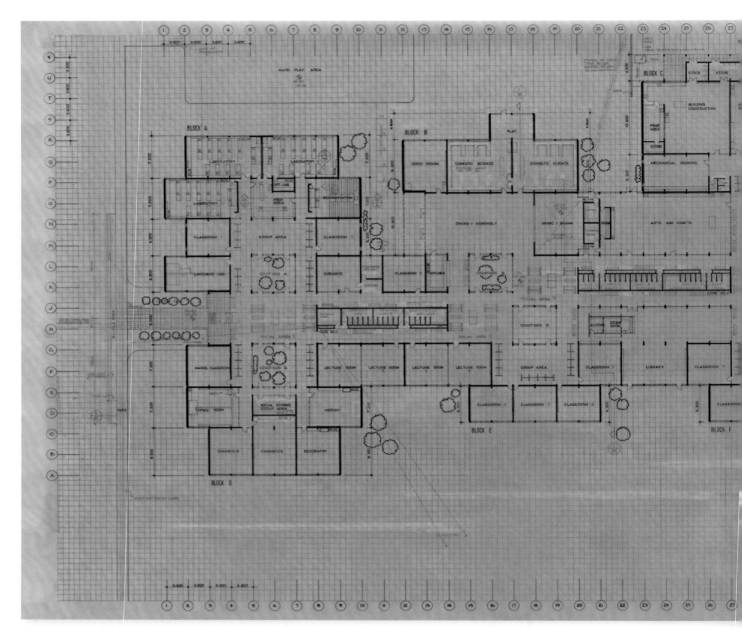

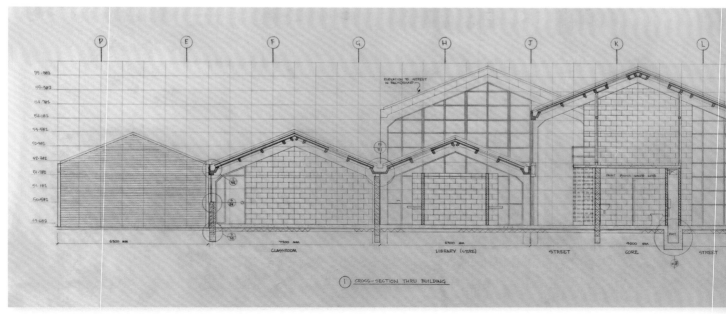

1 CROSS-SECTION THRU BUILDING

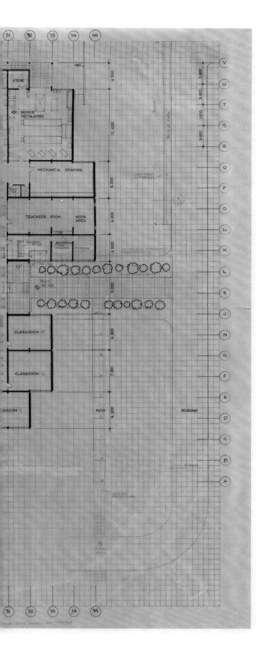

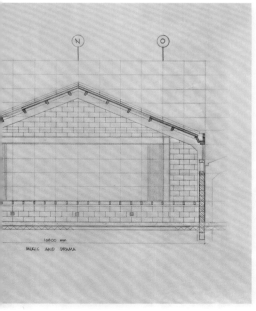

The refurbishment of Modernist buildings while retaining the values of the original design, particularly in relation to social ideals, is a challenge in an era of late-capitalism. **Aoibheann Ní Mhearáin and Tara Kennedy,** both architects and academics, present an analysis of the research conducted with Queen's University Belfast and John McLaughlin Architects on St Brendan's Community School in Birr, Ireland. Funded by a Getty Foundation 'Keeping It Modern' grant, the research explored how to conserve and retain Modernist buildings while respecting the social aspirations of the original design.

Modern architecture had as a core tenet the advancement of social ideals, and is now recognised as 'one of the defining artistic forms of the 20th century'.[1] The Getty Foundation's 'Keeping it Modern' grant, awarded in 2018 to St Brendan's Community School in Birr, County Offaly, in Ireland, funds research that guides the conservation of significant buildings of this period. The research team, led by Queen's University Belfast working with John McLaughlin Architects, aimed to establish the building's significance using a multi-strand method that encompasses historical, material, social and environmental investigations. This approach widens out the established conservation valuing process to include user experience and building fabric performance, blurring the boundaries between historical investigation and post-occupancy evaluation. The result creates a value matrix that reflects the wide spectrum of the building's life and positions social value at the core of future decision-making.

Peter and Mary Doyle Architects,
St Brendan's Community School,
Birr, County Offaly, Ireland,
1979

above left: The grid orders the programmed spaces, creating a nonhierarchical mat plan. The 'street' runs the length of the plan with courtyards distributed along it and classrooms surrounding the perimeter.

left: The section shows the precast-concrete portal frame system developed for the project. It was composed of three different column heights and varied rafter lengths, allowing for nine different bay widths from 3.6 to 10.8 metres, providing (roughly 12 to 36 feet) significant flexibility to the plan, with a simple technical means.

Emerging from radical new policies on education from the 1960s, St Brendan's was designed by Peter and Mary Doyle Architects for a 1974 Department of Education competition. The prototypical school design was built on the edge of Birr, a town in the middle of Ireland, and completed in 1979. Its nonhierarchical 'mat plan' embodied principles of democratisation and secularisation – a social agenda that was realised through the use of cheap, readily available technology and was responsive to the conditions in 1970s Ireland, 'a small, not very wealthy social democracy.'[2] Typical of contemporaneous construction, however, the design did not consider prime energy usage, and the school is therefore part of a wider 20th-century legacy of thermally inefficient, deteriorating buildings now at risk. In continuous use as a school for 900 pupils since it opened in 1980, the conservation of this concrete-frame structure encapsulates the environmental challenges of the 21st century. It opens up questions about the conservation of modern architecture in terms of identifying and interrogating what we value and why.

Typical of contemporaneous construction, however, the design did not consider prime energy usage, and the school is therefore part of a wider 20th-century legacy of thermally inefficient, deteriorating buildings now at risk

John McLaughlin Architects,
Landscape and place,
St Brendan's Community School,
Birr, County Offaly, Ireland,
2019

While the competition entry had no specified site, the system-built construction and original peat-burning heating technologies embed the school within the mass-produced landscape of the industrially harvested peat bog as well as the agricultural lands of County Offaly.

st. brendan's
community school

BIRR
CO. OFFALY

A Multilayered Methodology

The research has brought together multiple layers of analysis to understand the school's history and daily life. Baseline historical study included archival exploration and oral histories. To understand the performance of the building fabric and material vulnerabilities, consultants undertook condition surveys and opening-up work as well as considerable environmental data modelling and monitoring. Typical classroom and breaktime spaces were fitted with temperature, relative-humidity and air-quality monitors to record the daily fluctuations in use. In addition, sound analysis, thermography, air-pressure testing, thermal bridge analysis and condensation risk analysis helped to form a picture of the spaces under different conditions and parameters. Social survey methods including walking interviews, film and photography, were employed to capture the continuous life of the school. Paired 'then and now' photographs do not show decay, but uncover 40 years of wear and tear, of adaptation and piecemeal solutions to issues with its built fabric. As well as portraying ephemeral and temporal aspects of the school – the play of light and the ebb and flow of hundreds of young people – the images serve as analytic documents, revealing alterations.

Built inexpensively using local materials, the social life of St Brendan's was central to the design. The building simultaneously shapes and supports social structures and, in the description by former Principal Tom Foley, gives permission 'for things to happen that couldn't happen in an ordinary space'; in the social spaces 'the kids feel liberated'.[3] To further understand the lived experience, students were asked to make photographic responses to a set of questions about St Brendan's. These included capturing where they feel comfortable and uncomfortable, and how they perceive their school building. A map of the resulting images shows the value they give to social spaces where they feel comfortable, particularly the social 'street', which for them represents the spirit of the school.

View of the interior
social space,
2018

Taken nearly 40 years after the building opened, this photo shows the same volume and transparency of the original design, with the portal frames clearly expressed. Though there are some changes to the fabric, the core elements and qualities remain intact.

Built inexpensively using local materials, the social life of St Brendan's was central to the design

John McLaughlin
Architects,
Viewpoints of
students' photos,
St Brendan's
Community School,
Birr, County
Offaly, Ireland,
2019

opposite: The map shows the viewpoints of students' photographs that creatively record how they perceive their school. The images correlate with other information giving central importance to the social street.

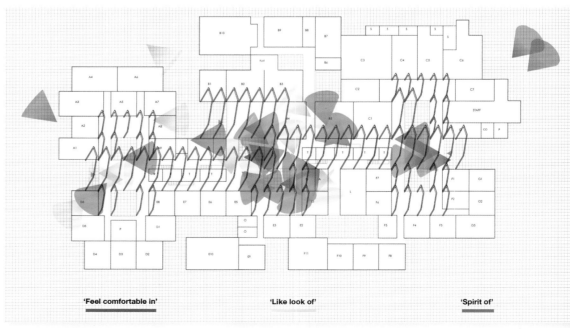

'Feel comfortable in'   'Like look of'   'Spirit of'

View of the school from
the entrance gate,
1980

In this photograph, taken shortly
after the building was opened, the
building is seen in its landscape
context, with the iconic service tower
in the background. Evident also is
the system-based construction of
portal frames that allows for different
volumes across the school.

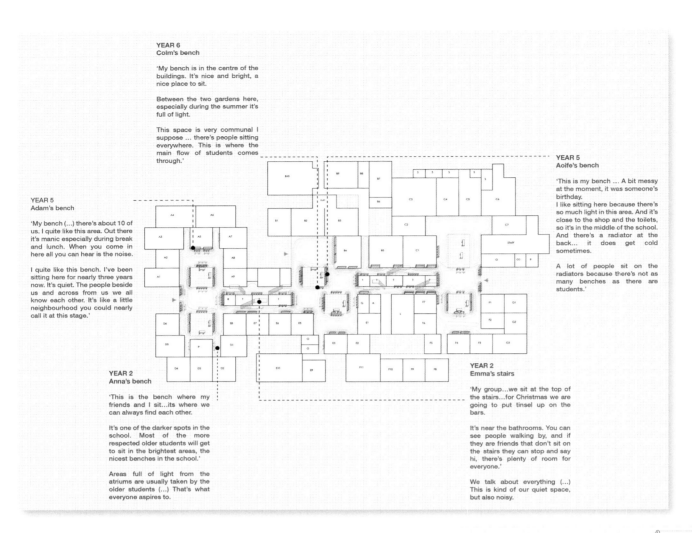

YEAR 6
Colm's bench

'My bench is in the centre of the buildings. It's nice and bright, a nice place to sit.

Between the two gardens here, especially during the summer it's full of light.

This space is very communal I suppose ... there's people sitting everywhere. This is where the main flow of students comes through.'

YEAR 5
Aoife's bench

'This is my bench ... A bit messy at the moment, it was someone's birthday.
I like sitting here because there's so much light in this area. And it's close to the shop and the toilets, so it's in the middle of the school. And there's a radiator at the back... it does get cold sometimes.

A lot of people sit on the radiators because there's not as many benches as there are students.'

YEAR 5
Adam's bench

'My bench (...) there's about 10 of us. I quite like this area. Out there it's manic especially during break and lunch. When you come in here all you can hear is the noise.

I quite like this bench. I've been sitting here for nearly three years now. It's quiet. The people beside us and across from us we all know each other. It's like a little neighbourhood you could nearly call it at this stage.'

YEAR 2
Anna's bench

'This is the bench where my friends and I sit...its where we can always find each other.

It's one of the darker spots in the school. Most of the more respected older students will get to sit in the brightest areas, the nicest benches in the school.'

Areas full of light from the atriums are usually taken by the older students (...) That's what everyone aspires to.

YEAR 2
Emma's stairs

'My group...we sit at the top of the stairs...for Christmas we are going to put tinsel up on the bars.

It's near the bathrooms. You can see people walking by, and if they are friends that don't sit on the stairs they can stop and say hi, there's plenty of room for everyone.'

We talk about everything (...) This is kind of our quiet space, but also noisy.

Tracking the design of the social spaces from the Doyles' earliest sketches presents an interesting picture of how this 'shearing layer' of 'stuff' might be valued and conserved

John McLaughlin Architects,
Shearing layers,
St Brendan's Community School,
Birr, County Offaly, Ireland,
2019

This new 'map drawing', developed from the original planometric by Peter and Mary Doyle, shows the shearing layers of the building and expresses the overlapping of the social and technical dimensions of the school.

John McLaughlin Architects,
Social heat map, St Brendan's
Community School, Birr,
County Offaly, Ireland,
2019

below: This plan shows the location of activity that radiates from seating in the social areas. Original benches designed by the Doyles are most prized, with additional benches and appropriated seating on radiators and stairs also hosting student groups.

The research (literally and figuratively) draws out how the technical performance and social life of the building overlap, in order to communicate how the technical impacts on the social and vice versa

This layered approach records how the school is used, and also critically how the building is perceived by its users. Drawing then became a means to bring the various surveys into the same frame. In the words of Gilles Deleuze and Félix Guattari: 'Make a map, not a tracing.' This 'has to do with performance, whereas the tracing always involves an alleged "competence".'[4] New maps of St Brendan's present intangible and subjective performative aspects of daily school life alongside technical analysis. The research (literally and figuratively) draws out how the technical performance and social life of the building overlap, in order to communicate how the technical impacts on the social and vice versa.

Matter and Meaning

The research team's work approaches the conservation of St Brendan's in a landscape where built environment is ever more heavily regulated. Walking a line between the imperfect 'cheapness' of the school and the possibility of its generous social spaces, it explores and exposes the lived experience of the building, its performance, in order to reframe its value and speculate on its future. With the view that it is important to 'care for things not because they produce value, but because they already have value',[5] the project prioritises the conservation of function alongside fabric.

For example, within the social spaces, seating plays a vital role. Benches, described by students as like 'little neighbourhoods',[6] host everything from homework to birthday parties. Although additional generic furniture has been added, the Doyles' original painted timber and blockwork benches remain the most sought after, prized based on their proximity to daylight, shops and toilets. Mapping these and tracking the design of the social spaces from the Doyles' earliest sketches presents an interesting picture of how this 'shearing layer' of 'stuff'[7] might be valued and conserved.

To cross-pollinate the multiple values of architectural history, social and technical performance, and functional and cost parameters, an outcome of this work is a matrix that provides a route to both understand and guide future actions as energy requirements become more stringent. The matrix will allow for the development of collated and aggregated data which overlays the subjective and objective, the social and the technical, making the case for conserving the school as a vital framework for social life into the future. ⌂

Notes

1. The Getty Foundation, 'Keeping it Modern': www.getty.edu/foundation/initiatives/current/keeping_it_modern/.
2. John O'Regan, *The Architecture of Peter and Mary Doyle: 1970–1990*, Gandon Editions (Dublin), 1990, p 7.
3. Interview with Aoibheann Ní Mhearáin, 13 August 2018.
4. Gilles Deleuze and Félix Guattari, *A Thousand Plateaus: Capitalism and Schizophrenia*, University of Minnesota Press (Minneapolis, MN), 1987, p 12.
5. Shannon Mattern, 'Maintenance and Care: A Working Guide to the Repair of Rust, Dust, Cracks and Corrupted Code in Our Cities, Our Homes and Our Social Relations', *Places Journal*, November 2018: https://placesjournal.org/article/maintenance-and-care/.
6. Adam Harte, fifth-year student at St Brendan's, interview with Tara Kennedy, 29 November 2018.
7. Stewart Brand, *How Buildings Learn: What Happens After They're Built*, Penguin (London), 1995, pp 12–23.

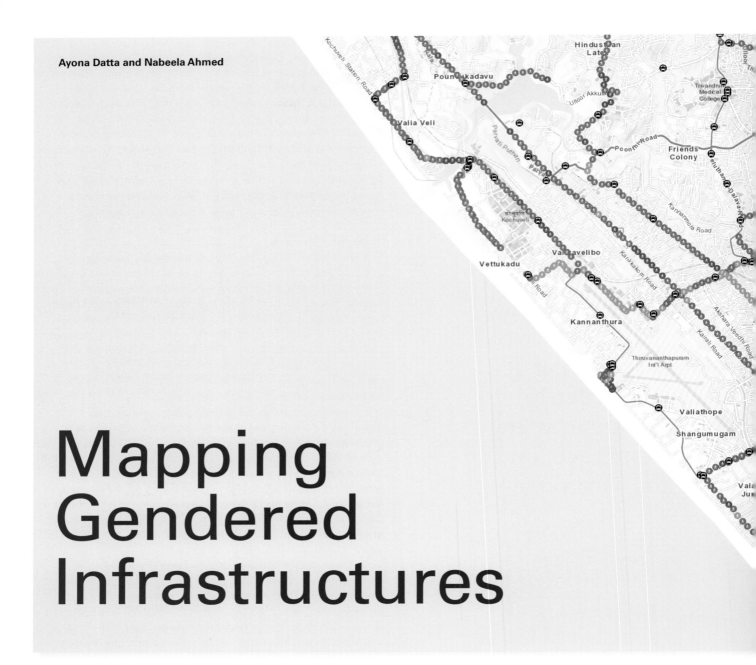

Ayona Datta and Nabeela Ahmed

Mapping Gendered Infrastructures

Critical Reflections on Violence Against Women in India

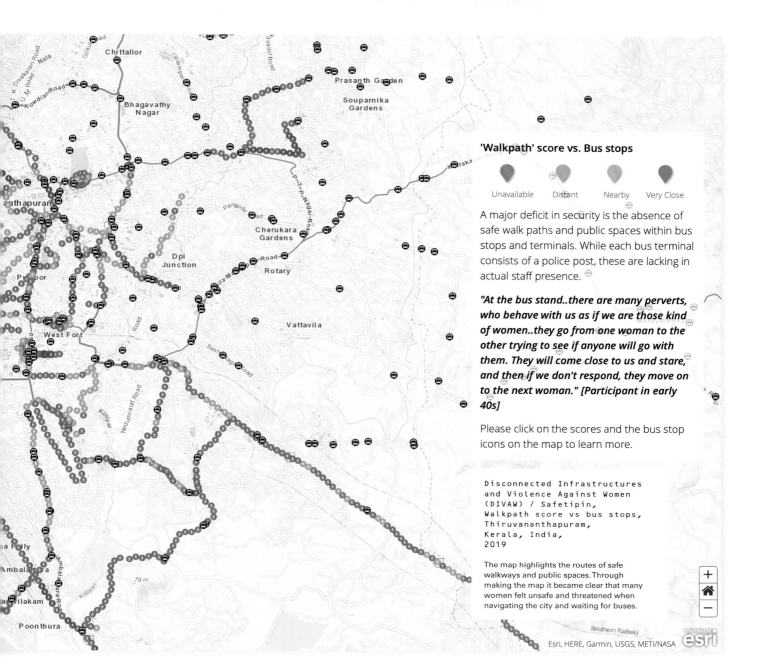

'Walkpath' score vs. Bus stops

| Unavailable | Distant | Nearby | Very Close |

A major deficit in security is the absence of safe walk paths and public spaces within bus stops and terminals. While each bus terminal consists of a police post, these are lacking in actual staff presence.

"At the bus stand..there are many perverts, who behave with us as if we are those kind of women..they go from one woman to the other trying to see if anyone will go with them. They will come close to us and stare, and then if we don't respond, they move on to the next woman." [Participant in early 40s]

Please click on the scores and the bus stop icons on the map to learn more.

Disconnected Infrastructures and Violence Against Women (DIVAW) / Safetipin, Walkpath score vs bus stops, Thiruvananthapuram, Kerala, India, 2019

The map highlights the routes of safe walkways and public spaces. Through making the map it became clear that many women felt unsafe and threatened when navigating the city and waiting for buses.

Esri, HERE, Garmin, USGS, METI/NASA

Using geographical information systems and participatory mapping with women from low-income areas of Thiruvananthapuram, Kerala, India, revealed their fears of violence against them, but equally the spatiotemporal 'dark spots' where this might occur. This in turn influenced infrastructure policy and provoked the introduction of a 'she corridor'. Ayona Datta, a professor of geography at University College London, and Nabeela Ahmed, postdoctoral research fellow at the Sheffield Institute of International Development, tell us how.

Maps are all around us. They tell stories of our world that are social, political, technological and temporal. They help us understand the world through the eyes of those who produce them. Maps are therefore loaded with the power of: (a) vision – how we imagine the world; (b) cartography – how we see and represent the world; and (c) practice – how we then act upon this. When maps exclude the visions and aspirations of women, make their spaces and times invisible, they inform policies that deny women and marginal communities a right to the city.

This article illustrates the stories that maps can tell us when they are produced through critical reflection, through participatory processes involving women users of space, and through the representation of everyday spatiotemporal experiences of fear and safety in Thiruvananthapuram, Kerala, India. The findings are based on a British Academy-funded research project based at King's College London and titled 'Intimate Infrastructures: Disconnected Infrastructures and Violence Against Women',[1] which had three aims: to map physical, digital and social infrastructures to reveal 'blind spots' of violence against women (VAW) in the city in order to inform urban policy, design and practice; to empower women from low-income neighbourhoods by improving their knowledge of and safe access to infrastructure in the Indian city; and to generate and communicate data that effectively mediate women's right to infrastructure with the safe city. Drawing upon the broader findings, this article critically maps the hotspots and blind spots of violence in the city and their connections to physical (such as public transport, lighting and toilets), digital (such as network connectivity, mobile phones and storage) and social (such as family/friends, law enforcement, institutional capacity) infrastructures in the city. It suggests that women in low-income neighbourhoods are exposed to increased violence (physical, emotional and sexual) in navigating the city if these three types of infrastructures are disconnected. Since infrastructures are gendered in their use and experience, their absence, failure or disconnectedness is a form of 'infrastructural violence'[2] – a 'process of marginalisation, discrimination and exclusion that operate through and are sustained by infrastructure' which deny women the right to safely inhabit or navigate the city.

Mapping gendered infrastructures involves a multiscalar study of how women living in low-income settlements experience and navigate physical, digital and social infrastructures from the home to the city. At the scale of the city, a mobile application called Safetipin Nite[3] was used to collect images taken from a moving automobile at every 50 metres across the city streets, which were then coded by programmers using nine parameters – lighting, footpaths, visibility ('eyes on the street'), openness, security, access to public transport, gender diversity, density of people (crowds) and feeling of safety. These parameters were overlaid on public infrastructure data – bus stops, police stations and public toilets – to produce rich geographic information system (GIS) maps. At the scale of the low-income neighbourhood, participatory mapping exercises with the women identified infrastructure blind spots and the spatiotemporality of violence in public spaces. This was supplemented with transect walks, ie systematic walks with the project team along a defined path (such as a participant's daily journey

Disconnected Infrastructures and Violence Against Women (DIVAW) / Visual Voice, Project diagram highlighting that urban infrastructure is made up of physical, digital and human dimensions, 2019

The Intimate Infrastructures: Disconnected Infrastructures and Violence Against Women project, based at King's College London, took its starting point in focusing on how physical and digital factors influence women's experiences of the city.

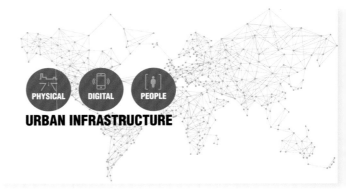

Chalai Bazaar Road, Trivandrum, Thiruvananthapuram, Kerala, India, 2019

In order to study how the visions and aspirations of women might inform policies, the Intimate Infrastructures project conducted fieldwork at Trivandrum, Kerala.

Mapping gendered infrastructures involves a multiscalar study of how women living in low-income settlements experience and navigate physical, digital and social infrastructures from the home to the city

to work), to generate in-depth knowledge of women's everyday experiences with(out) public infrastructures and in public spaces. At a household scale, the project team conducted a series of in-depth interviews and mental mapping exercises with the women to understand their daily experiences with infrastructure and VAW across public and private realms. This information was then geolocated and mapped alongside the wider city-level data above to highlight gendered infrastructures and VAW in Thiruvananthapuram.

Thiruvananthapuram as a 'Safe City'
While Kerala has passed inclusive and gender-sensitive legislation and policies in recent years, several challenges remain. Overall, there exists a huge data gap as well as a lack of awareness of the infrastructural contexts that impact on gender safety. Moreover, institutional capacity to implement gender equality strategies is weak due to limited general awareness and a gap in terms of skills and capacity to respond to and to develop concrete policies. In 2014, Thiruvananthapuram was included in India's 100 Smart Cities initiative under which it proposed to add CCTV surveillance, smart lighting, bus stops with Wi-Fi hotspots and an Integrated Command and Control Centre. A national law was passed in 2017, to make panic buttons and inbuilt global positioning systems (GPS) mandatory in all new mobile phones, while police in several cities – including Thiruvananthapuram – pushed smart safety apps for women to download to their smartphones. In Thiruvananthapuram, there was also a significant initiative to facilitate a 'safety corridor' between two women's colleges in the city centre, although this has not yet materialised. These initiatives however displayed a lack of understanding of the very real fear of and actual violence in the form of sexual harassment and assault that women faced in the city and in their homes and neighbourhoods.

Mapping Urban Infrastructures
A series of GIS overlays across Safetipin parameters and public infrastructure data, some of which are reproduced here, along with personal accounts of the women, suggest that while access to infrastructure does not necessarily preclude violence, the lack of access to infrastructure can reinforce existing forms of structural, material or symbolic violence for women in disadvantaged groups.

One map (pp 108–9, top) shows the Safetipin scores on security – based on proximity of police or security guards in each street. This is scored mostly 'None' as shown by the red hotspots. When overlaid with public data on police stations, it shows that even proximity to police stations does not make much difference to security.

Another map (pp 104–5) shows that the city is predominantly scored with poor walkpaths during evening hours and these are poorly correlated with the locations of bus stops. The high male presence in public spaces in the evening also aligns with local social norms that discourage women from leaving the house. The red and orange hotspots show how roads lack safe walking space to access infrastructure such as public transport, suggesting poor attention to gender-inclusive planning.

In addition to literacy and quality of mobile phone devices, there is also a geographic divide in digital infrastructures when the distribution of mobile networks is mapped across the city. Network coverage of the city at large is very poor, particularly outside the central zone. When there is coverage, this is often intermittent and sporadic – resulting in dropped calls, slow download speeds and crashed apps. This is particularly poignant in the context of pushing safety apps that rely on the network to be effective. Furthermore, very few women in low-income neighbourhoods use smartphones, or have the digital capacity to install and use these apps effectively.

A further map shows the overlay of the narratives of violence faced by women across the city against the location of the 'she corridor' (which is shown below right). Violence in this context is spatiotemporal and widespread across the city's public spaces. It is particularly poignant however that the route of the safety corridor discounts the ubiquitous nature of violence against women and focuses on a narrowly defined version of safety across two women's colleges.

Violence in this context is spatiotemporal and widespread across the city's public spaces

Disconnected Infrastructures and
Violence Against Women (DIVAW) /
Visual Voice,
The Digital Divide,
2019

Across India there is a digital divide, which means that women are far less likely to have either access to the Internet or a mobile phone than their male counterparts.

Disconnected Infrastructures and Violence Against Women (DIVAW) / 'She corridor', Thiruvananthapuram, Kerala, India, 2019

The map shows the location of a 2-kilometre (1.2-mile) 'she corridor' which was established in 2017. The road features security features such as CCTV and public toilets, breastfeeding centres and safe footpaths to improve accessibility.

Disconnected
Infrastructures
and Violence Against
Women (DIVAW) /
Safetipin, 'Security'
score vs police
stations,
Thiruvananthapuram,
Kerala, India,
2019

The map shows how participants'
feelings of safety correspond
spatially to proximity to police
stations. Green represents high
feelings of security and red none.

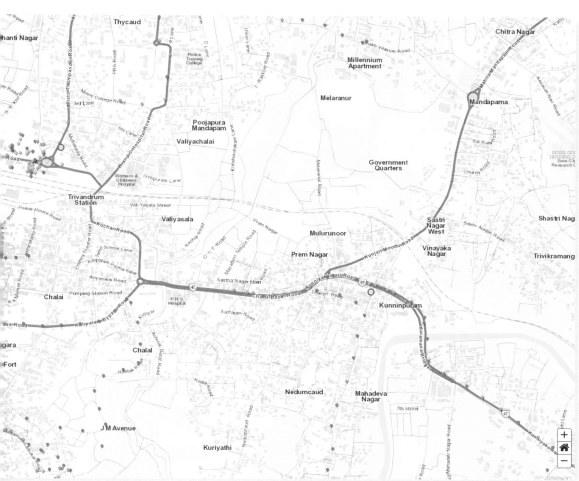

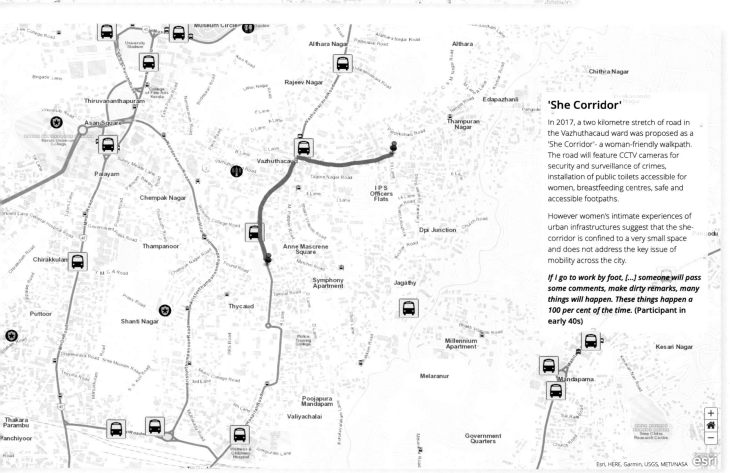

'She Corridor'

In 2017, a two kilometre stretch of road in
the Vazhuthacaud ward was proposed as a
'She Corridor'- a woman-friendly walkpath.
The road will feature CCTV cameras for
security and surveillance of crimes,
installation of public toilets accessible for
women, breastfeeding centres, safe and
accessible footpaths.

However women's intimate experiences of
urban infrastructures suggest that the she-
corridor is confined to a very small space
and does not address the key issue of
mobility across the city.

*If I go to work by foot, [...] someone will pass
some comments, make dirty remarks, many
things will happen. These things happen a
100 per cent of the time. (Participant in
early 40s)*

Esri, HERE, Garmin, USGS, METI/NASA

Participatory Mapping with Women in Low-income Neighbourhoods

Participatory mapping with a group of women living in a low-income neighbourhood reveals a much more complex story of the entanglements of infrastructure and VAW. In three 'mental maps' generated by women participants, they narrated their everyday routes in and out of their neighbourhood to approach the city. Transect walks, women's safety audits and mapping as participatory and feminist research methods[4] enable understanding of how women embody and perceive both affective and material barriers to infrastructures from the home to the city. The mental maps suggest how social infrastructures of family and public institutions are crucial to producing 'infrastructural violence'[5] wrought by disconnected gendered infrastructures. They highlight that while it is important that women have access to physical and digital infrastructures, it is only in the context of supportive social settings of family, community and public institutions (such as law enforcement) that this access can become 'safe' and empowering.[6] Broken or absent social infrastructures meant that women expressed deeply embedded fears and disinclinations to even go out on transect walks with the project team. Their mental maps suggested that violence against women is not only in actual physical or sexual violence – rather, violence is present in the immobility of women that confines them to their homes, forced to accept often abusive domestic relationships.

The illustrated map of the neighbourhood represents stories by the women regarding places and infrastructures they consider safe or unsafe. On the one hand, since the city has expanded, it is close to some of the important commercial and retail districts, yet these are largely male-dominated spaces. Women in low-income neighbourhoods have lower mobility than men – they are confined to the neighbourhood or places nearby. Yet even within the neighbourhood, women's access to public places such as the main road or the public pond is limited, since these are dominated by the presence of men engaged in drug and alcohol abuse.

In this context, women focused on the infrastructures present at their doorsteps, such as blocked drainage and sewage collected outside their houses, which increased their time-burdens and domestic labour, and which they perceived as another form of violence against women brought on by infrastructural failure. Participatory mapping became a process rather than a mere product which enabled women to represent their spatial knowledge, to critically reflect upon their experiences and articulate what they considered a safe environment. The participatory mapping process represented ways of knowing, navigating and seeing the city that challenge the urban planning- and technology-based approaches which focus on violence as incidents detached from the contexts in which they emerge.

Critical Reflections on Violence

Urban planning and design as disciplines are often accused of being gender-blind[7] because they produce policies and masterplans that do not consider the ways that women and marginal groups live in, navigate and experience the city. This is crucial particularly in the context of VAW where 'top-down' masterplans made by built-environment professionals

Chalai market,
Trivandrum,
Thiruvananthapuram,
Kerala, India,
2019

Crowdedness across the city largely overlaps with high male presence. So, women shopping in the local market do not necessarily feel increased safety as a result of the presence of people.

Community Pond,
Trivandrum,
Thiruvananthapuram,
Kerala, India,
2019

Women understand that their lack of access to water, sanitation facilities, drainage and energy violate bodily norms of thirst, hygiene, health and wellbeing and therefore act as intimate violence.

construct safety as a surveillance issue to be 'fixed' by improving technology. While technological advancements are important, a crucial slippage in this approach is the assumption that violence against women is an 'event' that can be addressed by improving 'response' times.

This article shows that violence is a complex assemblage of social, political and infrastructural blind spots in planning and governance of cities that have disempowered women from lower-income groups for decades and over generations. Women in low-income groups, historically left out of decision-making and participatory approaches to planning, 'see' and experience the city in much more spatiotemporal ways. Their experiences are often internalised and passed down as patriarchal family ideologies. Violence is routine, pervasive and cyclical between day and night perpetuated by family, neighbours and strangers alike. This understanding of violence should be central to questions of *who* maps the city at *what* scale and *how*. Taking a multi-scalar approach to mapping will develop narratives that are embedded within the contexts of women's everyday and intimate experiences of infrastructure and safety across household, neighbourhood and city scales. ⌀

Notes

1. https://disconnectedinfrastructures.wordpress.com.
2. Dennis Rodgers and Bruce O'Neill, 'Infrastructural Violence: Introduction to the Special Issue', *Ethnography*, 13 (4), 2012, pp 401–12.
3. www.safetipin.com.
4. Yasminah Beebeejaun, 'Gender, Urban Space, and the Right to Everyday Life', *Journal of Urban Affairs*, 14 (3), 2017), pp 323–34.
5. Rodgers and O'Neill, *op cit*.
6. Ayona Datta, 'Another Rape? The Persistence of Public/Private Divides in Sexual Violence Debates in India', *Dialogues in Human Geography*, 6 (2), 2016, pp 173–7.
7. Elizabeth L Sweet and Sara Ortiz Escalanate, 'Bringing Bodies Into Planning: Visceral Methods, Fear and Gender Violence', *Urban Studies*, 52 (10), 2015, pp 1826–45.

Taking a multi-scalar approach to mapping will develop narratives that are embedded within the contexts of women's everyday and intimate experiences of infrastructure and safety across household, neighbourhood and city scales

Anthony Hoete

THE HOUSE AS ANCESTOR

A TALE OF MĀORI SOCIAL VALUE

Hinemihi o te Ao Tawhito
(Hinemihi of the Old World),
Te Wairoa, Rotorua,
New Zealand,
1880s

The photograph was taken by the Burton Bros prior to the Mount Tarawera
eruption of 10 June 1886 when the meeting house was buried. The first
whare whakairo (carved meeting houses) were built in the mid-19th
century at a time of social upheaval (the Treaty of Waitangi, Christianity,
disease). Māori 'architects' responded by applying carvings to *whare* to
represent the *mana* (life force) of the community.

In order for a house to have social value, it must be a focus of spiritual, political and cultural significance to a specific community. This is a tale of one such house, the Māori *whare*. The *whare* is formally greeted as one would a person, before addressing the humans within. Carving, ornament and pattern constitute most of its Māori-ness, and are central to its place in Māori civilisation. **Anthony Hoete**, founder of WHAT_architecture, unravels the architecture of Māori placemaking, its social standing and worldview.

When Māori arrived in Aotearoa (New Zealand) in the early 14th century, such was the magnitude of the voyage that this indigenous society remained in isolation for the next 300 years. The Māori classical period was one of remote distillation that created a society distinct from other eastern Polynesian cultures. In Māoritanga (Māori-ness), the recounting of tradition was activated through myriad social forms including *waiata* (song), *kapa haka* (dance), *whakairo* (carving) and *moko* (tattooing). With the notable absence of writing, speech flourished: Te Reo (Māori language) is first and foremost an oral literature. The *pepeha*, for example, is a means of spoken introduction through which Māori establish their identity, a story of their connection to *moana* (sea), *waka* (canoe), *maunga* (mountain), *awa* (river), *whare* (house), *marae* (public space), *iwi* (tribe) and *hapū* (community). With the arrival of European settlers in the late 18th century, Māoritanga has been perpetually reshaped by increasing urbanisation and closer contact with New Zealanders of European descent (Pākehā). To offset identity loss, much social value is afforded to the revival of traditional practices, and the *whare* remains the key socio-spatial actuator.

Waterscape not Landscape

The surface area of Polynesia is so vast that it is one and a half times larger than Europe and, down there, all that is solid is swamped by liquid a thousand times over. Furthermore, a thousand tiny islands are sprinkled over this oceanic triangle, which reaches to Hawaii in the north, Rapa Nui in the east and New Zealand in the south. The earliest migratory patterns were therefore sea based, and of relatively small social clusters. There were, and still are, no Polynesian cities in the European sense. Given the solitude that is the architecture of the archipelago, traditions carried by written words could be readily washed away in one capsizing wave. Books as jetsam. *Waiata* would thus carry oral traditions forward in a not too dissimilar manner to the sea shanty. Through identification to a *waka*, one could trace descent from one of the great fleet of migratory canoes, departure from (is)lands of no return and arrival in Aotearoa. Within the indeterminate liquid context that is the sea, space and time are easily lost. Fact and fiction became blended, and so the constant retracing of one's lineage (*whakapapa*) remains the narrative that underpins Māori society today.

Ancestral stories recount the house as a boat. During the day the canoe could be used for fishing, whilst upturned at night it could shelter. In Polynesian mythology the sequence of house-or-canoe is a chicken-or-egg causality dilemma: the Samoans claim the house was built first, whereas the Tongans posit the canoe.[1] In Hawaiiki, sails are floor mats and canoe/houses are lashed together. Forever tied, house building is predicated upon boat building, and vice versa.

Yet the traditionally adorned modern plan-form of the *whare* only emerged after European arrival. Referred to as a 'meeting house', a *wharenui* served as a forum for discussion at a time when Māori were experiencing much social upheaval relating to land loss, politics and religion. With its formal emphasis on the front facade – gabled roof form, singular fenestration – it was often interpreted by Western scholars as being crude. The Māori *whare* today needs to be understood in the same way we greet another person.[2] Much like the traditional Māori greeting – the *hongi*, or nose press – the architectural arrangement is a *kanohi ki te kanohi* (or face-to-face) engagement. When formally speaking on the *marae*, one then talks to the house before addressing those in attendance. From a Western perspective, talking to a building, like Doctor Doolittle talking to the animals, might be considered madness.[3] Yet it is not appropriate to apply a Western perspective, with its seemingly well-intended heritage practices, to indigenous culture. A visitor to a *marae* would thus be expected to acknowledge and greet the host's meeting house as part of the introduction: '*E te whare e tū nei, tēnā koe*'. Many *whare* are named after ancestors and are regarded as their outstretched body. The *tekoteko* is a gabled head and is the face of the ancestor, the *maihi* (bargeboards) their arms, the *kūwaha* (door) a mouth, the *tāhuhu* (ridge pole) a spine, and the *heke* (rafters) ribs. Each house has its own social meaning accumulated over time through use. Until recently,[4] Māori architecture did not exist in academic studies, as architecture was deemed to be non-indigenous, an import arising from Eurocentric lineages. Paradoxically, however, though Māori architecture had been suppressed, Māori *whare* had been exported since the 19th century. Today, four *whare* are located outside New Zealand. Three of these are cryogenically frozen as part of internal museum collections, but one is still in use as a house: Hinemihi o te Ao Tawhito (Hinemihi of the Old World).

Hinemihi o te Ao Tawhito
(Hinemihi of the Old World),
Clandon Park,
Surrey, England,
2012

In 1891 the Governor of New Zealand, the 4th Earl of Onslow, wanted a souvenir of the country to take back to England. The Hinemihi *whare* was thus sold and shipped to the UK in 1893, although it is questionable as to whether there really was a 'willing buyer' or 'willing seller' given the social upheaval Māori were experiencing at the time.

above: The figuratively carved elements of the *whare* are personifications of particular ancestors and resemble the human body in structure. The *tekoteko* represents the head and is a carved, human-like figure crafted to instil guardianship over the tribe.

below: The Māori *whare* has just one window. Hinemihi was originally built with an English sash window and thus incorporated European building elements before she arrived in the UK.

opposite: Carving is of the pane, a triangular profiled part of the ridge beam that lies over the front porch. The supporting rafters, or *heke*, represent the ribs of the ancestor.

A WHAT architecture depiction of Hinemihi envisaged without ornament. Whilst her carvings (*whakairo*) constitute less than 5 per cent of her materiality, they constitute more than 95 per cent of her Māori identity. Without them Hinemihi is merely a grass hut.

The National Trust's announcement in 2019 of its support for the exchange of her deteriorating carvings for newly created carvings of original dimensions, with motifs to be informed and inscribed by both British and New Zealand stakeholders, is a final affirmation of the social value that resides within the Māori *whare*

The original six-panel side-hung door to Hinemihi was also European, although many *whare* were built with leftward-sliding cavity doors (and right-sliding cavity windows).

The internal central post supports the ridge pole of a Māori meeting house. The naturalistic style of the carved figure was intended to emphasise the social side of the ancestor.

A House in Two Places at Once

Her story is one of transience. Carved in 1881, Hinemihi was originally built in the village of Te Wairoa near Lake Rotorua prior to the eruption of Mount Tarawera in 1886. Having provided shelter to a fortunate few (including one of her carvers, Tene Waitere), she was then shopped and shipped by the New Zealand Governor General of the time, Lord Onslow, to the UK in 1891 as garden exotica for Clandon Park near Guildford in Surrey. Without any accompanying erection documentation, Hinemihi was reconstructed, albeit chopped and chipped, as a boat shed until recuperating soldiers from the Māori Pioneer Battalion discovered her in 1917 and, sensitive to her deteriorating physical state, relocated her opposite Clandon House, *kanohi ki te kanohi*. As a colonial face-off this arrangement symbolically mirrors the historic, and at times confrontational relationship between Pākehā and Māori in the colonisation of New Zealand. Yet the siting of Hinemihi in the garden of Clandon House could also be read as positively transformative: today the grass lawn also serves as *marae ātea* (a rural form of public space specific to the South Pacific). The lawn allows for the traditional ritual of *pōwhiri* (welcome) and thereby anchors Hinemihi's shifting space to her new place. She has sat there for the greater part of her life. Hinemihi now has two meaningful historic settings: one trace to New Zealand and the shore of Lake Tarawera; another to the UK in Clandon Park. Thanks to the social value Māori attribute to the meeting house, she can now be in two places at once.

In Aotearoa, tribal narratives continue to reference the absent Hinemihi in speech as the ancestress of the *hapū* and as a means by which to recall and consolidate *whakapapa*. Despite the radical changes to the socioeconomic landscape of the UK over the past 130 years, Hinemihi continues to resonate with a distinctly Māori cultural identity. As an exemplar project of future heritage, she represents a social space that connects two distant lands. A partnership between both places, and the exchange of knowledge and materials, has imbued her with her dual timeframes: her past as Hinemihi o te Ao Tawhito (old world) and her future Hinemihi o te Ao Hou (new world). The National Trust's announcement in 2019 of its support for the exchange of her deteriorating carvings for newly created carvings of original dimensions, with motifs to be informed and inscribed by both British and New Zealand stakeholders, is a final affirmation of the social value that resides within the Māori *whare*. ᴐ

Notes

1. Michael Austin, 'Pacific Island Migration', in Stephen Cairns (ed), *Drifting: Architecture and Migrancy*, Routledge (New York), 2004, pp 224–36.
2. Bill McKay, 'Maori Architecture: Transforming Western Notions of Architecture', *Fabrications*, 14 (1 & 2), December 2004, pp 1–12.
3. Michael Linzey, 'Speaking To and Talking About: Maori Architecture', *Interstices 1: Journal of Architecture and Related Arts*, 1990, pp 49–60.
4. Deidre Brown, *Maori Architecture: From Fale to Wharenui and Beyond*, Raupo Penguin (Auckland), 2009.

Walk
With
Us

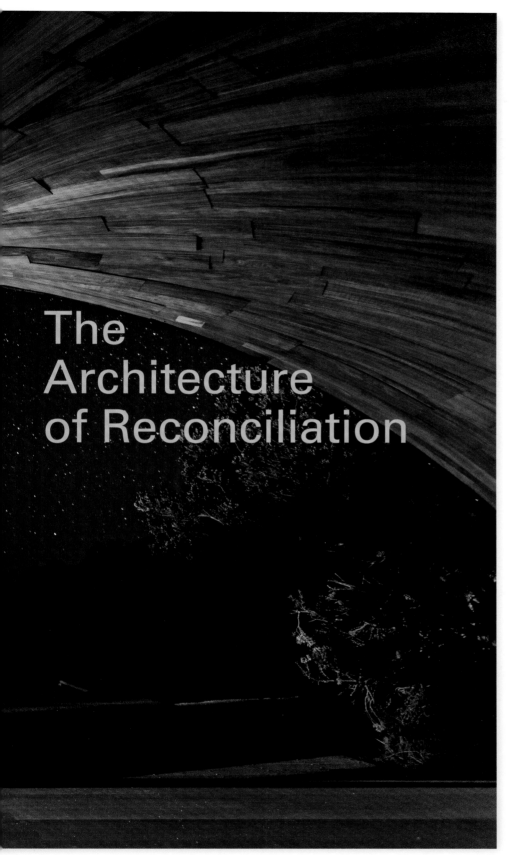

The
Architecture
of Reconciliation

Mat Hinds

Taylor and Hinds Architects,
krakani lumi,
wukalina—Mount William National Park,
Tasmania,
2018

The circular firepit anchors gathering and
storytelling under a vast and ancient night sky –
the canvas from which the palawa-pakana
Creation is told. Krakani lumi is a place made
for the telling of the ancient and continuing
story of Tasmania's first peoples.

Krakani lumi is a small eco-tourism development on a site of deep cultural importance to the Aboriginal people of Tasmania. It is a vehicle for land return, conceived as a place of restful calm to contemplate the landscape and partake in its rituals. Architect **Mat Hinds** describes its architectural constitution and spatial significance as a place of reconciliation for both Aboriginal and non-Aboriginal communities alike.

Taylor and Hinds Architects,
krakani lumi,
wukalina–Mount William National Park,
Tasmania,
2018

Krakani lumi – 'place of rest' – is a remote eco-tourism project, located in the traditional cultural homelands of the palawa-pakana, the first peoples of lutruwita (Tasmania). Designed by Taylor and Hinds Architects, and completed in 2018, it is a series of individual timber pavilions, including a communal building that incorporates gathering spaces, a shared kitchen, stores and ablutions, and six individual sleeping huts that accommodate non-indigenous guests on an Aboriginal-guided multi-day walk through Tasmania's remote North East coastal plains. A site of deep cultural significance and a site of dispossession, the Country[1] that surrounds krakani lumi is redolent of the palawa-pakana Creation story. Within this context, krakani lumi acts both as a vehicle for land return, and as a social setting for reconciliation between non-indigenous and Aboriginal peoples within an ancient cultural landscape.

Encounter
In 1831, during the period now known as the Black War, a promise of treaty was offered to the Coastal Plains Nation chieftain Mannalargenna by the 'friendly' conciliator George Augustus Robinson, who acted as envoy of the Colonial Government of Van Diemen's Land (later Tasmania). On the offer of salve, and protection for his war-exhausted people, Mannalargenna agreed to temporarily depart from his homeland. He died in exile, three weeks later, on a remote island mission, and was buried with 300 other men, women and children who had been systematically dispossessed of their lands and culture. Mannalargenna's descendants have fought for decades for the return of the tribal lands upon which promises of treaty were made. At the centre of the expanse of these coastal plains rises a single hillock, known traditionally as wukalina (Mount William). Krakani lumi is located at the foot of this sacred site.

Enveloped deep within a grove of coastal heath, the charred timber-clad communal pavilion emerges as a shadow from the scrub.

above: On approach, the shimmering charred hardwood exterior of the communal pavilion belies the cultural interior. The materials were detailed to allow seasonal occupation and robust, taut forms.

below: After a 'Welcome-to-Country' ceremony, Aboriginal guides open the main pavilion, revealing the cultural interior to guests. The revelation is symbolic of the agency afforded to the Aboriginal people in the telling of their story. Borrowing from an ancient spatial tradition of the palawa-pakana, the sense of interiority expands out into the cultural landscape.

The traditional shelters of Tasmania's first peoples were sophisticated structures, carefully sited and well made, and layered to a greater or lesser degree of enclosure. Typically, the exterior was sheathed in a weathering skin of broad sheets of bark, while the interiors were lined in tiers of softer paperbark.[2] Upon these interior vaults, the Country was redrawn, interweaving storytelling and shelter.[3]

At the inception of the project, the Taylor and Hinds team were taken by elders Clyde Mansell and Graeme Gardner to an ancient sacred site – made over hundreds of generations by their ancestors – where they were told the palawa-pakana Creation story. The telling of the Creation is a speaking-into-being of Country – an initiation into the spiritual and cultural interior of the landscape. This context and the notion of the story-telling interior is an important *parti* for krakani lumi.

Cultural Landscape, Interiority and Spatial Agency

The social intentions of architecture coalesce in plan. Robin Evans writes that 'if anything is described by the architectural plan, it is the nature of human relationships'.[4] The protection and revelation of the cultural interior is a primary spatial idea in krakani lumi, and commences as a carefully choreographed encounter within the broader site.

Guests approach from a pristine dune, just south of a freshwater creek, through open coastal heath that is rich in diverse flora and animal life. Impossible to see before arrival, krakani lumi is enveloped deep within a grove of silver banksia. Clad entirely in charred Tasmanian hardwood, the individual structures of the standing camp appear as a series of discrete, dark pavilions, merging as shadows into the surrounding dense scrub and camouflaging the camp when it is not in use. The exteriors are robust, tautly and economically detailed, and resilient to the sea air and to tampering. There is no glass.

Guests arrive on to a large deck where a circular firepit is centrally placed to anchor gathering and story-telling. A fire is lit by Aboriginal guides, and a Welcome-to-Country is conducted in which guests are doused in white plumes of eucalyptus-infused smoke, and daubed with red ochre. A series of large sliding doors are opened to reveal a blackwood-lined apse, proportioned to the earliest accounts of traditional communal domes, and acting as a proscenium to the telling of the Creation that follows.

To the north of the main building, the individual sleeping huts are all sited in particular relationships with the dense coastal heath. When open, a warm half-domed blackwood-lined interior is exposed.

The interiors of the huts are directly proportioned to the earliest accounts of palawa-pakana shelters. The floor is fully mattressed. and bedding is supplemented by wallaby pelt throws. Guests wake to honeyeaters feeding just beyond the reach of their beds.

The individual sleeping huts are positioned in particular relationships with the surrounding coastal heath. Timber awnings conceal the privacy of the interior, and focus the view towards the ground – as an active plane of experience of the site.

Clad entirely in charred Tasmanian hardwood, the individual structures of the standing camp appear as a series of discrete, dark pavilions

These social and cultural intentions are offered by krakani lumi through a series of emblematic spatial and material narratives

Constructed almost entirely from Tasmanian hardwoods, the interior details express the methodology of making, and reference cultural forms and motifs such as the half-moon and circle.

There is no glass at krakani lumi. Light and exposure is moderated by a series of sliding panels and solid timber awnings.

Concealing and Revealing

In his essay 'Say Goodbye to the Colonial Bogeyman' (2005), Hugh Webb writes:

> If Aboriginal people are enclosed then they can reverse that enclosure, 'rebuilding the walls of the enclosure in new ways, changing its internal environment, making it easier or more difficult for non-Aborigines to visit ....' They can – through the appropriation and abrogation of dominant codes – reverse the searchlight of racial surveillance.[5]

Just as an apse opens to the vault of a larger nave, the interiors of krakani lumi reconfigure the experience of the landscape as a larger room. The exterior charred 'skin', which conceals and protects the narrative of the cultural interiors, ensures agency to the Aboriginal community in the telling of their story. When revealed, a sense of expanding interiority magnifies the immersion with the surroundings, and the privileged custodial and kinship encounter with Country is instantiated.

This notion of concealing and revealing is dialectically at odds with the mainstream spatial tradition in contemporary Australian architectural discourse, which seeks to dissolve the threshold and gaze upon the landscape. The notion of Country is socio-spatially intrinsic, where communal identity is manifest out of the interiorised cultural and social body of the land itself. These social and cultural intentions are offered by krakani lumi through a series of emblematic spatial and material narratives.

In the communal pavilion, sliding wall panels and shutters moderate internal light and exposure, and subtle tectonic references to cultural motifs are echoed in the interior detailing and timber work. Between the domed interior lining and charred exterior, nests are provided for hollow dependant marsupials and birds, including the endangered New Holland Mouse that frequents the site. Within the individual sleeping huts, bedding is supplemented with wallaby pelt throws – known traditionally as reore[6] – and guests wake to soft morning light and the activity of honeyeaters feeding just beyond the reach of their beds.

Architecture is an 'atavistic urge', as Marcel Breuer put it, of a constant return to origins.[7] So too it is an act of constant remembrance. This sense resolves most strongly when the attention of architecture is focused towards the essential nature of shared human experience. It is a quality architects must strive for to occasion human being and togetherness. ∆

Notes
1. For a detailed definition of the term, see Bill Gammage, *The Biggest Estate on Earth: How Aborigines Made Australia*, Allen & Unwin (Sydney), 2012, p 139.
2. Henry Ling Roth, *Aborigines of Tasmania*, Cambridge University Press (Cambridge), 2009, p 108.
3. NJB Plomley (ed), *Friendly Mission: The Tasmanian Journals and Papers of George Augustus Robinson, 1829–1834*, Queen Victoria Museum & Art Gallery (Launceston, Tasmania), 2008, p 548.
4. Robin Evans, 'Figures, Doors, Passages', *Translations from Drawing to Building and Other Essays*, Architectural Association (London), 1997, p 56.
5. Hugh Webb, 'Say Goodbye to the Colonial Bogeyman: Aboriginal Strategies of Resistance', *Altitude*, 6 (Reading Indigenous Australian Texts Part 2), 2005: https://thealtitudejournal.files.wordpress.com/2008/07/71.pdf.
6. Roth, *op cit*, p 109.
7. Marcel Breuer, 'Matter and Intrinsic Form', transcript of lecture at the University of Michigan, Smithsonian Institution Archives of American Art, 1963, p 4: www.aaa.si.edu/collections/marcel-breuer-papers-5596/subseries-6-1/reel-5718-frames-1092-1183.

Against a Convenient Mediocrity

A Word from
Δ▷ Editor Neil Spiller

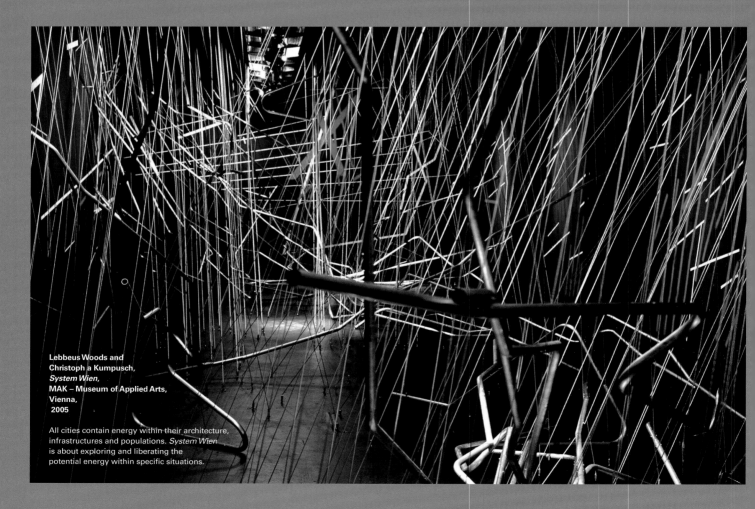

**Lebbeus Woods and
Christoph a Kumpusch,
System Wien,
MAK – Museum of Applied Arts,
Vienna,
2005**

All cities contain energy within their architecture,
infrastructures and populations. *System Wien*
is about exploring and liberating the
potential energy within specific situations.

[Lebbeus Woods] combines a faith in the ability of advanced technology to open new worlds to all mankind with a belief that such brave new worlds can only exist in the actual act of construction and will reconstitute the community of mankind.
— Aaron Betsky[1]

The 'social value' theme of this $\triangle$ is important, however a different emphasis might be the social value of the ill-defined – the free, the non-proscribed and the resistant. Here the focus will be on American architect Lebbeus Woods and his collaborator Austrian architect Christoph a Kumpusch, exploring their creative friendship and mutual support, and the works that came out of this alliance as an illustration of a different type of social value.

These included their contributions to 'The Snow Show' (2003–6), where the two also worked with German-American artist Kiki Smith, and Kumpusch's thesis project Alien Automaton (2005), conducted at the Cooper Union School of Architecture in NewYork, under Wood's tutelage.

Firstly, however, we must explore some of the concepts and intellectual points of departure of Woods' work – preoccupations that stayed with him throughout his lifetime. During the 1960s, he met and became friends with the inventor of second-order cybernetics, Heinz von Foerster. Second-order cybernetics asserts that human interaction with our world is reflexive and often beyond our own creative control. It is full of elision and illusion, feedback and readjustment, depending on the system and its observers/collaborators. Further, second-order cyberneticists acknowledge that we make our worlds by interacting with them and that they are all different, exceptional, particular and personal. Woods' architecture and drawings are strange, unconventional, and leave the viewer/user to figure out how they might inhabit such spaces – an idea he called 'freespace',[2] linking back to those initial encounters with Von Foerster.

Coupled with freespace is Woods' notion of 'resistance'. In 2009 he wrote a seminal and witty text entitled 'Architecture and Resistance', in which he states that 'Living changes us, in ways we cannot predict, for the better and the worse. One looks for principles, but we are better off if we control them, not the other way around. Principles can become tyrants, foreclosing on our ability to learn. When they do, they, too, must be resisted.'[3] He went on to make a long list of what he believed architects should resist, including buying a car and moving to Los Angeles, but also some important advice on resisting the accepted nature of architecture and its social relationships:

Resist any idea that contains the word algorithm ...
Resist the idea that architecture is a building ...
Resist the idea that architecture can save the world ...
Resist people who are satisfied ...
Resist the assertion that architecture is a service profession ...

Resist believing that anyone knows what will actually happen ...[4]

Collaboration and the fluidity of ideas was another important key to the world of Lebbeus Woods, and a string of accomplices including Mas Yendo, Dwayne Oyler and Hani Rashid worked with him. Kumpusch was the last, and a strong bond emerged between them. As Kumpusch writes, Woods 'never did want to be presented, re-presented or written about in a singular fashion. I think there was almost nobody out there that thought like this. Leb to a degree defined "collaboration" this was way before "collaboration" became a buzzword – and often an empty one.'[5]

Fields of Unknown Quantities
In 2002, as part of a response to the shock of 9/11, French philosopher Paul Virilio curated 'Unknown Quantity', an exhibition of differing artists' work at the Cartier Foundation, Paris.[6] The show featured Woods' and collaborator Alexis Rochas's installation The Fall, which consisted of a field of thin rods, intensely complex, poised to imply the collapse of the building it was housed in. A different point of departure for Woods, the narrative of the piece focused on the acceleration of gravity, and the brief moment when what is collapsing is still collapsing, before it becomes collapsed – a space of duality, and kinetic and potential energy. In short, a field of architectural possibilities.

In 2004 Woods described this move away from the object/building to the field as 'a shift I have made in order to liberate, in the first case, myself. If I cannot free myself from the reassurance of the habitual, how can I speak

Lebbeus Woods, Christoph a Kumpusch and Kiki Smith,
Contribution to 'The Snow Show',
Turin, Italy,
2006

The collaborative contribution to 'The Snow Show' illustrates Woods'
mastery of the curve and the line, forming a Woodsian mandala in the ice.

of the experimental … if I cannot free myself from obsession with the end-product'.[7]

At Cooper Union, Kumpusch remembers that 'halfway through that first Master's semester, about two weeks before midterms, Woods asked me if I wanted to work with him. There were no projects. None. But there we started'.[8] Kumpusch's final thesis work contains elements of Woods' work on *The Fall* in Paris and what would become a decade-long of collaborations: *The Snow Show* (2003–6), *System Wien* (MAK – Museum of Applied Arts, Vienna, 2005), *Martyrs* (Palazzo delle Papesse, Siena, 2007) and *Earthwave* (SCI-Arc Gallery and the Traction Triangle in Bloom Square, Los Angeles, 2009–13), culminating in the extraordinary *Light Pavilion* (2007–12) within Steven Holl's Sliced Porosity Block in Chengdu, China. All of the projects were influenced by their creators' interest in vectorial dynamics, reconfiguring spaces, non-orthogonal splinters of material and lines of force delimiting spatial thresholds, used and inhabited in new ways.

A contemplative intervention in the frozen landscape, the 'Snow Show' installation encourages introspection.

The House of Blue Light

'The Snow Show' was a creative experiment, a quest into the collaborative process through the drawings, photographs and models of teams of established and emerging artists and architects. It manifested itself in different guises in Venice and New York (2003), and pieces were built in Finland (2003 and 2004) and Turin (2006). Teams included Yoko Ono and Arata Isozaki; Cai Guo-Qiang and Zaha Hadid; John Roloff and Diller + Scofidio; Eva Rothschild and Anamorphosis; Do-Ho Suh and Morphosis; and Rachel Whiteread and Juhani Pallasmaa. Woods and Kumpusch were to work with artist Kiki Smith.

Culture, education, science and international dialogue were central to the aims of the show. The art exhibition included all these components, its curators believing that the world was seeking new directions in a turbulent time, and that historically, art had led the way. The collective 'Snow Show' was thus a timely, symbolic effort in the direction of harmony in a troubled world still suffering tremors after the fall of the Twin Towers.

In the Woods and Kumpusch installations, 'Leb's lines were realised by strands of fibre-optic lights submerged underneath three layers of ice. Streaks of light served as design and light source, revealing shadowy figures by Kiki Smith submerged below the surface, drawing the viewer's gaze into its depth.'[9] The optical-fibre light streaks resonate with Woods' previous projects and his indomitable, flowing drawing hand. So even with this economy of line and gesture, he evokes his resolute world. The cyclic, mandalic motif appears right at the beginning of his oeuvre and continued throughout his work, in different guises, over many decades.

The installation at 'The Snow Show' is also reminiscent of his swirling signature and often indecipherable notes on his drawings, figures from a barely known alphabet for a cybernetic future. Kiki Smith's floating figures, bathed in aquatic blueness, bring to mind another Woodsian trope, that of humanity looking searchingly out into the universe yet also delving deep within itself in quiet contemplation. Here the figures are in a chilled submersion tank.

Unknown Qualities of the Urban

Alien Automaton was the culmination of Kumpusch's studies with Woods at the Cooper Union: 'Leb donated the material to me as it was left over from his show at the Cartier Foundation in Paris, which he had shipped to New York. He did, however, tell me that my models could only use "physical joints".'[10] So the aluminium rods of *The Fall* became *Alien Automaton*. The project was for a series of interventions to facilitate entrances and access points to the then-derelict High Line in New York. 'Leb called it "Essay in Aluminium" – it was an urban story-telling device.'[11]

Christoph a Kumpusch,
Alien Automaton,
**The Cooper Union
School of Architecture,
New York City,
2005**

Kumpusch's thesis project
utilised salvaged aluminium
rods and channels from
Woods' earlier project *The Fall.*

Alien Automaton was a set of
geometric tools with which to
open up urban possibilities for
the then-derelict High Line in
New York.

All of the projects were influenced by their creators'
interest in vectorial dynamics, reconfiguring spaces,
non-orthogonal splinters of material and lines
of force delimiting spatial thresholds, used
and inhabited in new ways

A contemporary folly,
it is a place to experience for the fun of it, a place to
look out from and a place to look into

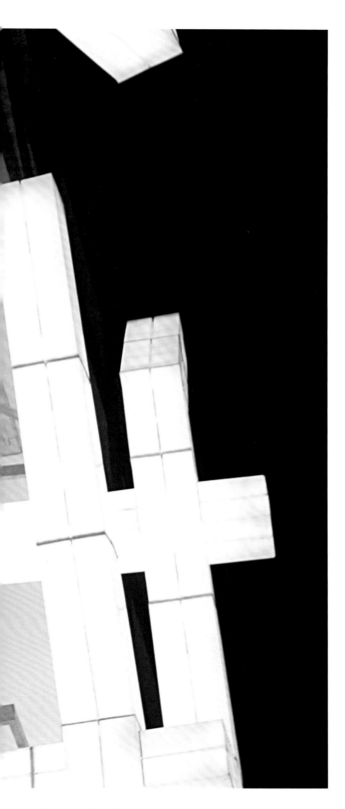

Alien Automaton is at once a drawing, sculpture and an architecture. It is simultaneously an intervention into the urban condition and also a kit of spatial tools with which to operate on the urban fabric. The project is an investigation into the architecturally possible: not prescriptive, but projective. Its suggestive nature is born out of its reconfiguration and its ability to imply spatial and structural connections, opportunities, thresholds and limits when juxtaposed in different situations and contexts – both interior and urban exterior.

The process is in effect a tactic to dislocate the architectural self. As architects we develop languages, tropes, formal and spatial architectural fetishes that we repeatedly use and which give us pleasure. *Alien Automaton*'s clue is in its title; it seeks out the different, the unworldly and the strange, and not a little danger. The 'Automaton' element is associated with the uncanny feeling of the machinic impersonating the fleshly. It also implies confederacy with the 'automatic writing' so beloved by the early Surrealists as a method to help them remove preconceived ideas and create new poetry and prose, again dislocating their creative selves to find new solutions. If one idea describes Woods' and Kumpusch's collaborative work it is this.

A Lebbian Last Word
Woods' and Kumpusch's collaboration reached its creative crescendo with the commission of the *Light Pavilion* in Chengdu. A contemporary folly, it is a place to experience for the fun of it, a place to look out from and a place to look into. It is in opposition to the rigid orthogonality of the rest of Holl's scheme, providing an emphatic exclamation mark.

At this point it is right to leave the last words to Lebbeus Woods himself: 'The moral lesson is that resistance … is best when it takes the high road of creative thinking, rejecting not so much this or that alternative, but any acquiescence to conventional thinking that yields a convenient mediocrity.'[12] ⌀

Notes
1. Aaron Betsky, 'Lebbeus Woods: Materialist Experiments and Experiences', in *Lebbeus Woods: Terra Nova, A + U*, extra edition, August 1991, p 8.
2. Lebbeus Woods, *ANARCHITECTURE: Architecture is a Political Act*, Academy Editions (London), 1992, pp 8, 11, 46 and 50.
3. Lebbeus Woods, 'Architecture and Resistance', 9 May 2009: https://lebbeuswoods.wordpress.com/2009/05/09/architecture-and-resistance.
4. *Ibid.*
5. Email to the author, 5 November 2019.
6. Paul Virilio, *Unknown Quantity*, exh cat, Thames & Hudson (London), 2003.
7. Stephanie Carlisle and Nicholas Pevzner, 'Exhibit: Lebbeus Woods at The Drawing Center', *Scenario Journal*, 13 June 2014: https://scenariojournal.com/exhibit-lebbeus-woods-at-the-drawing-center/.
8. Email to the author, 5 November 2019.
9. Email to the author, 12 November 2019.
10. *Ibid.*
11. *Ibid.*
12. Lebbeus Woods, 'Thoughts on Architecture of Resistance': www.lebbeuswoods.net/LW-ResistanceText2.pdf.

Lebbeus Woods and Christoph a Kumpusch,
Light Pavilion,
Sliced Porosity Block,
Chengdu, Sichuan province, China,
2007–12

Housed within Steven Holl's Sliced Porosity Block, the *Light Pavilion* is the culmination of Woods' and Kumpusch's work together. It uses preoccupations of light, energy and the non-orthogonal to create a beacon of joy to be explored.

Nabeela Ahmed is a postdoctoral research fellow at the Sheffield Institute of International Development (SIID) at the University of Sheffield. She is a critical geographer focusing on precarity, gender and labour in urban settings in the global South, and developing innovative participatory methodologies for understanding these themes. She completed her PhD in 2018 at the University of Sussex, and worked as a postdoctoral research associate for the British Academy-Funded project 'Disconnected Infrastructures and Violence Against Women' at King's College London.

Nicola Bacon is the co-founder of the Social Life enterprise, which focuses on place-based innovation and social sustainability. Until July 2012 she was the Young Foundation's Director of Local and Advisory Projects. She has worked across sectors, in the UK government, as director of a youth homelessness charity, and as Director of Policy at housing charity Shelter. She is a Young Foundation Fellow, a fellow of the Academy of Urbanism, a Design Council Built Environment Expert and a mentor for Bethnal Green Ventures. She is also a member of the Brent Design Advice Panel.

Irena Bauman is a practising architect and a founding director of Bauman Lyons Architects and of start-up fabrication company MassBespoke. She developed the MassBespoke digital fabrication system with Matt Murphy at Bauman Lyons Architects with the support of three Innovate UK research grants. She is currently the holder of the Royal Commission 1851 Fellowship 2018–2019, developing business models for the Built InCommon neighbourhood-based housing fabrication workshops.

Ayona Datta is a professor in the Department of Geography, University College London (UCL) researching gender citizenship, urban futures and smart cities in the global South. She is author of *The Illegal City: Space, Law and Gender in a Delhi Squatter Settlement* (Ashgate, 2012), and co-editor of *Translocal Geographies: Spaces, Places, Connections* (Ashgate, 2011) and *Mega-Urbanization in the Global South: Fast Cities and New Urban Utopias* (Routledge, 2016). She is editor of the *Urban Geography* journal and on the editorial boards of *Antipode, Digital Geography and Society* and *EPD: Society and Space*.

Cristina Garduño Freeman is an early career academic focused on understanding, evaluating and designing for people's connection with places. Her research contributes to the fields of architectural history, critical heritage and digital humanities through the discourses of reception, place attachment, social value and participatory culture. She is the author of the book *Participatory Culture and the Social Value of an Architectural Icon: Sydney Opera House* (Routledge, 2018). She has also practised professionally in architecture, landscape architecture and urban design, and in visual communication design.

Paul Goodship is a data scientist at Atkins, where he models and analyses built-environment data. Until the beginning of 2019 he worked for Social Life as a researcher, focusing on placemaking in London. In 2018 he completed a PhD in urban morphology and socio-spatial analysis within the Space Syntax Laboratory at University College London (UCL). His thesis explored the role of spatial connectivity in the upgrading process of informal settlements, and how this transformation alters local commercial and movement activities, researched through the case of Medellín, Colombia, and its urban cable-car intervention.

Kerry Harker is the founder and Artistic Director of the East Leeds Project. She was formerly co-founder and Artistic Director at The Tetley, a contemporary art space in the city. She is also currently a final-year PhD candidate in the School of Fine Art, History of Art and Cultural Studies at the University of Leeds, where her research considers artist-led initiatives in the UK's visual arts sector since the 1990s.

Mat Hinds is a Tasmanian-based architect and the founding director of Taylor and Hinds Architects, which he established with Poppy Taylor in 2013. He has held lecturing positions at his alma mater, the University of Tasmania, since 2009. In 2019 he was a juror for the Australian Institute of Architecture National Architecture Awards programme. Through original and strategic design thinking, Taylor and Hinds has established a national reputation for context-specific work that is conceptually rigorous, tectonically refined and functionally considered. In 2018, its krakani lumi eco-tourism project in Tasmania was awarded the Best Building in the Asia-Pacific at the INDE Design Awards.

Anthony Hoete is the founder of WHAT_ architecture based in East London. Editor of the spatial mobility book *ROAM* (Black Dog Publishing, 2004), his practice-based research Game of Architecture posits that architecture today is a much-contested field of guidelines and regulations. In order to thwart professional marginalisation and to change the game, architects must be active in both rule disruption through interrogation and interpretation, and change their role through increasing adaptability. To this end, the Game of Architecture Ltd is now acting as managing contractor and developer in the construction of a newbuild residential block in Peckham.

Tara Kennedy practises and teaches architecture, with expertise in collaborative public projects, engaging with a wide range of organisations and institutions. She graduated with a Master's in architecture from University College Dublin (UCD) in 2013. She also has a BA in sculpture from the National College of Art and Design, Dublin. Working with John McLaughlin Architects since 2014, she coordinated the 'Making Ireland Modern' centennial exhibition in 2016. In 2008 she co-founded the practice Culturstruction, and was also a co-founder of the community-based design organisation Commonage. She was co-curator of Free Market, the Irish Pavilion at the 2018 Venice Architecture Biennale. She is a lecturer at the Cork Centre for Architectural Education.

Karen Kubey is an urbanist specialising in housing and health, and a Faculty Fellow in Design for Spatial Justice at the University of Oregon. She is the guest-editor of ᗄ *Housing as Intervention: Architecture Towards Social Equity* (July/August 2018), and served as the first executive director of the Institute for Public Architecture. Holding degrees in architecture from the University of California, Berkeley and the Columbia University Graduate School of Architecture, Planning and Preservation (GSAPP), she began her career as a designer of below-market housing. She has received support from the New York State Council on the Arts and the MacDowell Colony.

Jateen Lad is an architect based in Manchester, UK and Pondicherry, India. His work is guided by a belief that good architecture and ethical construction practices can be a force for social change. He set up in the aftermath of the 2004 Indian Ocean tsunami and brings a holistic approach integrating bespoke architecture, environmental design, construction management and the delivery of buildings in a socially empowering manner – often in challenging contexts where design skills are most needed.

Mhairi McVicar is a Reader at the Welsh School of Architecture, Cardiff University, and is Academic Lead of Community Gateway, a platform that facilitates long-term partnership projects between the university and the city's Grangetown district. Following BSc studies in the UK and a US Master's, she practised in Chicago and worked on architectural projects in London and the Orkney Islands. Her research examining the pursuit of architectural quality within the processes of professional architectural practice has been published in *Architectural Research Quarterly*. She is the author of the book *Precision in Architecture: Certainty, Ambiguity and Deviation* (Routledge, 2019).

Aoibheann Ní Mhearáin is a practising architect and academic. She was educated at the UCD School of Architecture and Princeton University, and is Associate Director at John McLaughlin Architects. She is an assistant professor at the UCD School of Architecture, Planning and Environmental Policy. Her essay on St Brendan's Community School in Birr, published in *InfraÉireann: Infrastructure and the Architectures of Modernity in Ireland* (Ashgate, 2015) provided the starting point for the Getty-funded research on the school, which she has been co-ordinating since its award in 2018. She was a participant in the 2018 Venice Biennale in the group exhibition 'Close Encounters'.

Jenni Montgomery is the Business Development Director at Barton Willmore, the largest independent planning and design consultancy in the UK. Her role includes identifying market challenges and growth opportunities, and driving innovation that enables all aspects of the practice to respond to these. She has been intrinsic in the Greenkeeper development programme from the successful, original bid for grant funding, to commercialisation and preparation for launch in 2020. Greenkeeper lies at the heart of Barton Willmore's approach to urban and new settlement planning and design, but the collaborative approach has allowed all to benefit from emerging methods at the forefront of social value measurement.

Edward Ng is an architect and Yao Ling Sun Professor of Architecture at the School of Architecture of the Chinese University of Hong Kong. He specialises in green building, environmental and sustainable design, and urban climatology for city planning. In early 2014, noting the cultural and socioeconomic needs of remote villagers in Southwest China, he established the One University One Village initiative to continue his humanitarian work with his students. He believes that knowledge creates the future, and it is the responsibility of academia to chart this future.

Constantin Petcou is an architect and semiologist, and a co-founding member and director of atelier d'architecture autogérée (aaa). He has coordinated numerous research, urban and architectural projects in the field of strategic design and participative architecture, including R-Urban, CivicLine and Wiki Village Factory. His work with aaa has been exhibited at the Museum of Modern Art (MoMA) in New York, the Venice Architecture Biennale, Pavillon de l'Arsenal in Paris and Canadian Centre for Architecture (CCA) in Montreal, and has received numerous distinctions and awards including the Building4Humanity prize for resilient building (2018), European Prize for Political Innovation (2017), Curry Stone Design Prize (2013) and European Prize for Public Space (2012).

Doina Petrescu is Professor of Design Activism at the University of Sheffield, and a co-founding member of atelier d'architecture autogérée (aaa). Her research concerns issues of gender, co-production, resilience and urban commons in relation to architecture. Her publications include *Architecture and Resilience* (2018), *The Social (Re)Production of Architecture* (2017), *Altering Practices: Feminist Politics and Poetics of Space* (2007) and *Architecture and Participation* (2005), all published by Routledge.

Peter Andreas Sattrup is a Danish architect, Senior Advisor on Sustainability at the Danish Association of Architectural Firms, and a board member of the Green Building Council Denmark and the Sustainability Work Group of the Architects' Council of Europe. He is dedicated to documenting and communicating how architecture creates social, environmental and economic value, and works with policymaking, innovation and development within the construction sector. He is the prize-winning lead author of *ARCHITECT – Document Your Value Creation*, a guide to how architects can document the value of their work and create new business opportunities.

Neil Spiller is Editor of *D*, and was previously Hawksmoor Chair of Architecture and Landscape and Deputy Pro Vice Chancellor at the University of Greenwich, London. Prior to this he was Vice Dean at the Bartlett School of Architecture, University College London (UCL). He has made an international reputation as an architect, designer, artist, teacher, writer and polemicist. He is the founding director of the Advanced Virtual and Technological Architecture Research (AVATAR) group, which continues to push the boundaries of architectural design and discourse in the face of the impact of 21st-century technologies. Its current preoccupations include augmented and mixed realities and other metamorphic technologies.

Li Wan is a research associate at the School of Architecture of the Chinese University of Hong Kong. She specialises in sustainable building design and assessment systems in poor rural areas of China. She is also a co-founder and the CEO of the One University One Village initiative. The team's rural projects have received numerous international awards including the UNESCO Asia Pacific Awards for Cultural Heritage Conservation, Terra Award, AR House Award and World Architecture Festival Building of the Year.

What is *Architectural Design*?

Founded in 1930, *Architectural Design* (△) is an influential and prestigious publication. It combines the currency and topicality of a newsstand journal with the rigour and production qualities of a book. With an almost unrivalled reputation worldwide, it is consistently at the forefront of cultural thought and design.

Each title of △ is edited by an invited Guest-Editor, who is an international expert in the field. Renowned for being at the leading edge of design and new technologies, △ also covers themes as diverse as architectural history, the environment, interior design, landscape architecture and urban design.

Provocative and pioneering, △ inspires theoretical, creative and technological advances. It questions the outcome of technical innovations as well as the far-reaching social, cultural and environmental challenges that present themselves today.

For further information on △, subscriptions and purchasing single issues see:

http://onlinelibrary.wiley.com/journal/10.1002/%28ISSN%291554-2769

Volume 89 No 4
ISBN 978 1119 506850

Volume 89 No 5
ISBN 978 1119 546245

Volume 89 No 6
ISBN 978 1119 546214

Volume 90 No 1
ISBN 978 1119 540038

Volume 90 No 2
ISBN 978 1119 555094

Volume 90 No 3
ISBN 978 1119 617563